Reading Nephi Reading Isaiah

PROCEEDINGS of the
MORMON THEOLOGY SEMINAR

The PROCEEDINGS OF THE MORMON THEOLOGY SEMINAR series is based on a novel idea: that Mormons do theology. Doing theology is different from weighing history or deciding doctrine. Theology speculates. It experiments with questions and advances hypotheses. It tests new angles and pulls loose threads. It reads old texts in careful and creative ways.

The Mormon Theology Seminar organizes interdisciplinary, collaborative, theological readings of Latter-day Saint scripture. Seminar participants with diverse backgrounds closely explore familiar texts in creative ways. In partnership with the Laura F. Willes Center for Book of Mormon Studies at the Neal A. Maxwell Institute for Religious Scholarship, the Mormon Theology Seminar presents these experiments upon the word to foster greater theological engagement with basic Mormon texts.

For more information, see mormontheologyseminar.org.

Series Editor

Brian M. Hauglid

Other MORMON THEOLOGY SEMINAR *books include:*

Adam S. Miller, ed., *An Experiment on the Word: Reading Alma 32*

Reading Nephi Reading Isaiah

2 Nephi 26–27

Edited by
Joseph M. Spencer
Jenny Webb

Second Edition

NEAL A. MAXWELL INSTITUTE *for* RELIGIOUS SCHOLARSHIP

Brigham Young University
Provo, Utah

A Proceedings of the Mormon Theology Seminar book
Neal A. Maxwell Institute, Provo 84602 | maxwellinstitute.byu.edu

First edition published 2011 by Salt Press. Second edition 2016.

Library of Congress Cataloging-in-Publication Data

Names: Spencer, Joseph M., editor. | Webb, Jenny, 1978– editor. | Mormon Theology Seminar. Proceedings of the Mormon Theology Seminar.
Title: Reading Nephi reading Isaiah : reading 2 Nephi 26-27 / edited by Joseph M. Spencer and Jenny Webb.
Description: Provo, Utah : Neal A. Maxwell Institute for Religious Scholarship, Brigham Young University, Utah, [2015] | ?2015 | Series: Proceedings of the Mormon Theology Seminar | Includes bibliographical references.
Identifiers: LCCN 2015050053| ISBN 9780842528665 (print : alk. paper) | ISBN 9780842529556 (epub) | ISBN 9780842529563 (kindle)
Subjects: LCSH: Book of Mormon. Nephi, 2nd—Criticism, interpretation, etc. | Bible. Isaiah, XXIX—Criticism, interpretation, etc.
Classification: LCC BX8627 .R365 2015 | DDC 289.3/22--dc23
LC record available at http://lccn.loc.gov/2015050053

∞ This paper meets the requirements of ANSI/NISO Z39.48-1992 (Permanence of Paper).

ISBN 978-0-8425-2866-5

Cover photograph: a portion of the *Great Isaiah Scroll* from Qumran. Original photograph by Ardon Bar Hama, courtesy of Wikimedia Commons.

Printed in the United States of America

Contents

Introduction

SAINT AUGUSTINE'S *CONFESSIONS*—a text that is itself a book-length prayer—opens with a series of difficult questions about the nature of prayer:

> Grant me, Lord, to know and understand whether a man is first to pray to you for help [or] whether he must know you before he can call you to his aid. If he does not know you, how can he pray to you? For he may call for some other help, mistaking it for yours. Or are men to pray to you and learn to know you through their prayers? Only, how are they to call upon the Lord until they have learned to believe in him? And how are they to believe in him without a preacher to listen to?[1]

That Augustine raises such complex and self-aware questions about prayer as he prays is significant. Indeed, it may only be in the act of praying that one can genuinely ask whether prayer is possible. Prayer, for Augustine, makes room for a particular kind of introspection, one that can question both the nature and function of prayer and the actions and intentions of the petitioner.

1. Saint Augustine, *Confessions*, trans. R. S. Pine-Coffin (New York: Penguin, 1961), 21.

The papers in this volume attempt to do something similar to what Augustine undertakes in his prayer. They ask what it means to read scripture and, crucially, they address this question through the actual work of reading scripture. In addition to the obvious role that scripture plays in the life of devotion, reading scripture can also give us room to pose questions both about the nature and function of scripture and about the relationship between the intentions of the text and the intentions of the reader.

Though scholarly in tone, the papers collected here do not reflect a "merely" academic approach to the Book of Mormon. Though they raise complex theoretical questions about what it means to read the Book of Mormon, they do so only as a by-product of their attempt to seriously engage Mormon scripture. And, by raising reflective questions about scripture *within the context of reading scripture itself,* they are grounded in an honest devotion to the texts. In short, while many of the questions addressed may appear academic, they are driven by pressing and practical commitments.

This volume is especially interested in asking what it means to read Mormon scripture in a Mormon context. To this end, the authors collectively selected a scriptural text that *both performs and comments on what it means to read scripture.* Second Nephi 26–27 is remarkable for doing precisely this. In these chapters, Nephi carefully reads the writings of Isaiah (specifically Isaiah 29) in a multifaceted process that involves copying, interpreting, contextualizing, repurposing, recontextualizing, and prophesying—often all at once. Nephi's own rereading of Isaiah's original text powerfully illuminates what it means to actively but faithfully engage in the difficult and unavoidably creative work of reading scripture.

Of course, this volume is hardly the first to ask about the place and function of Isaiah in Nephi's writings. Because Isaiah is generally regarded as a difficult author and because the Book of Mormon nonetheless endorses Isaiah's writings without reserve, there have been more books published over the years on Isaiah's role in the Book of Mormon than on any other major aspect of this New World book of scripture. However, where most of these publications aim at "making Isaiah easier" or at helping Latter-day Saints to "get through Isaiah," the essays in this volume arguably complicate Isaiah. These papers, rather than trying to speed things up, try to help readers slow down and get stuck in Isaiah long enough to consider what Nephi's own reading of Isaiah can teach us about reading scripture in general.

Given the complexity of the text under discussion (2 Nephi 26–27), it was clear that the chapters demanded, first of all, a close, careful, and extended reading. The Mormon Theology Seminar (http://mormontheologyseminar.org) provided us with an ideal setting in which to do this work.

The Mormon Theology Seminar is an independent, scholarly project that fosters short-term, collaborative seminars focused on reading and reporting about specific scriptural texts. These seminars provide a setting where a group of researchers can systematically work through a text, write and present papers based on their research at a public conference, and then organize those papers, along with a summary report of the group's findings, into a published volume.

With the support of the Mormon Theology Seminar, this seminar was organized under the title "Reading Nephi Reading Isaiah." Over the course of three months of collaborative analysis, we worked through the entire text. (The whole of this verse-by-verse, group analysis is available as a free PDF on the Seminar website.) We then presented our findings at a conference held on April 15, 2009, at Brigham Young University. The conference was jointly sponsored by the Mormon Theology Seminar, the Richard L. Evans Chair of Religious Understanding at Brigham Young University, and the Neal A. Maxwell Institute for Religious Scholarship. We are grateful for the support of these institutions, and we are pleased to present our findings in published form.

The contents of this volume can be categorized as follows. We begin with the Summary Report, a collaborative document designed to orient the reader to the overarching questions, themes, and conclusions that emerged from the seminar's discussions. As do all seminars sponsored by the Mormon Theology Seminar, ours began by formulating several key questions designed to focus our dialogue and organize its eventual findings. The Summary Report contains the seminar's tentative conclusions.

Following the Summary Report, we present the conference papers themselves. These papers, while the work of individual authors, developed out of the seminar discussions and exhibit the wide range of thought and interests provoked by the text.

Joseph Spencer's paper addresses an important preliminary question: what drew Nephi's attention to the writings of Isaiah in the first place? Through a detailed analysis of 2 Nephi 26:33–27:6, Spencer unearths a series of theological concerns shared by Nephi and Isaiah. Heather and Grant Hardy follow with a comprehensive overview of Nephi's editorial methodology in 2 Nephi 26–27. Comparing Nephi's handling of Isaiah 29 to Mozart's handling of a musical theme, they demonstrate the close and careful style of Nephi's interpretive work. Jenny Webb's contribution then explores some of the philosophical and theological implications of Nephi's interpretive methodology. Webb argues that Nephi's surprising refusal, in 2 Nephi 26–27, to attribute to their author the words he borrows directly from Isaiah serves as a key for making theological sense of Nephi's approach to reading scripture.

The remaining texts address in more detail the specifics of 2 Nephi 26–27. Julie Frederick takes up the image of the "seal" in the intertwined texts of Isaiah 29 and 2 Nephi 26–27. Asking the deceptively simple question of what Nephi has in mind with the word *seal*, Frederick demonstrates the effective impossibility of assuming merely physical or material referents for terms in Nephi's prophecy. George Handley, in turn, complicates the question of "metaphoricity" in Nephi's text and in scripture more generally. Handley examines how scriptural texts structurally "liken" themselves in a way that anticipates and invites later readers to actively do the same. Finally, Kimberly Berkey concludes the series by addressing the influence of 2 Nephi 26–27 in the larger text of the Book of Mormon. Taking a detailed look at Helaman 5, Berkey argues that Nephi's handling of Isaiah influenced the historiographic style of later authors and editors of the Book of Mormon.

Summary Report

1. How does Nephi adapt Isaiah's text, and what do his methods tell us about what it means to read a scriptural text?

To make sense of Nephi's use of Isaiah 29 in 2 Nephi 26–27, it is important to assume that Nephi, as a careful, conscientious author, incorporated Isaiah's text into his own with purpose and precision. Working from this assumption, we see that Isaiah 29 appears to function as the structural and thematic framework on which Nephi then hangs his own prophecies about the eventual destruction of his people, the emergence of the Book of Mormon, and the relationship between the Gentiles and the Lamanites.

The way Nephi handles Isaiah in 2 Nephi 26–27 differs, however, from the way he handles him elsewhere. A first indication of this uniqueness is the fact that Nephi in this case does *not* identify his Isaianic source. Elsewhere, extended quotations from Isaiah are prefaced and identified as such (e.g., 2 Nephi 11:2), but here no such textual markers are to be found. Further, while Isaiah quotations present elsewhere in Nephi's writings consist of entire chapters taken directly from Isaiah without added asides or commentary inserted by Nephi, 2 Nephi 26–27 not only divides up what it draws from Isaiah into distinct sections, it also contains a substantial amount of text written by Nephi himself. Indeed, Nephi's method here is one not of *duplication* but *adaptation*. In these chapters, Nephi deliberately and systematically repurposes Isaiah 29 to his own prophetic ends.

This adaptive methodology is illustrated in verses 16–17 from 2 Nephi 26. In what follows, the sections adapted from Isaiah 29 are italicized.

> 16 *For those who shall be destroyed shall speak unto them out of the ground, and their speech shall be low out of the dust, and their voice shall be as one that hath a familiar spirit* [Isaiah 29:4]; for the Lord God will give unto him power, that he may whisper concerning them, even as it were *out of the ground; and their speech shall whisper out of the dust.* [Isaiah 29:4]
> 17 For thus saith the Lord God: They shall write the things which shall be done among them, and they shall be written and sealed up in a book. . . .

Notice, here, how Nephi copies but cuts into Isaiah's text, working his own comments into Isaiah 29:4, and then adapts the text even further by framing 29:4 with his own prophecy in verse 17. Nephi weaves Isaiah's words into his own prophetic cloth. These textual weavings by Nephi are not straightforwardly an attempt to elucidate Isaiah's original intent and meaning. Instead, Nephi is explicitly recontextualizing and appropriating the language and imagery of Isaiah 29 in order to explain his own visions regarding the fate of Lehi's descendants. (For example, the verses just cited occur within the context of Nephi's prophecy regarding his own descendants, the Nephites.)

In a perhaps still more striking illustration of Nephi's freedom in adapting the text of Isaiah 29 to his own purposes, he transforms into two distinct events what in Isaiah 29 is clearly only one historical event. Language originally describing just the singular fall of Jerusalem is thus employed to describe both the ancient fall of the Nephite nation and the latter-day fall of the Gentile nations. Nephi accomplishes this curious appropriation by inserting into the middle of his quotation of Isaiah 29:5–6 a lengthy aside that contains no actual Isaiah text (verses 19–33 of 2 Nephi 26 and verse 1 of 2 Nephi 27). The aside thus serves as a textual break that traces the major temporal shift from the end of the Nephites (around 400 CE) to the arrival of the Gentiles in the New World (around 1500 CE). Though verses 5 and 6 of Isaiah 29 both refer to the same event, in Nephi's account the two verses are distributed among references to two intertwined but temporally distinct events.

As we observe Nephi's authorial methodology in action throughout 2 Nephi 26–27, we are given possible insight into Nephi's affection for Isaiah. Nephi views Isaiah's text as immensely rich. Rather than looking at the Isaiah text as the product of problematic and possibly multiple redactions—most modern scholars see Isaiah 29 as being composed of two separate texts and possibly by two separate authors—Nephi reads Isaiah prophetically, imposing unity, looking for patterns, and trying to see how the accidental tensions introduced through redaction might be theologically productive. Nephi allows the shape of Isaiah's text to give form and meaning to his own spirit of prophecy. Likening, in this sense, is a question of taking the material letter of the text as a kind of template for making sense of one's own experience and vision. This process is neither exegetical nor hermeneutic; rather, reading in this sense involves taking a past text as a guide for faithfully recasting the present.

Nephi's interactions with Isaiah model an important aspect of what it means to read scripture. For Nephi, to read scripture is to take up the text as a text and then rework it so that it reflects one's current understanding and vision as revealed through the spirit of prophecy. Reading scripture then becomes active rather than passive as each reader takes up the burden of his or her own prophetic responsibility.

2. What does 2 Nephi 26–27 tell us about the nature of prophecy and scriptural application?

Though Nephi often turns to Isaiah in his writings, it is only in 2 Nephi 26–27 that he does so in a way that allows the reader to closely analyze how he reads scripture. Elsewhere, Nephi tends to either quote Isaiah at length without providing any substantive commentary (see 1 Nephi 20–21; 2 Nephi 7–8; 12–24) or weave snippets from Isaiah's writings into his own prophecies (see 1 Nephi 22; 2 Nephi 6; 10; 25; 28–30).

In 2 Nephi 26–27, however, Nephi inverts the latter of his two usual approaches to Isaiah: there, rather than weaving snippets of Isaiah into his own prophecy, he weaves snippets of his own prophecy into a substantive text from Isaiah (specifically, Isaiah 29). Further distinguishing his work in 2 Nephi 26–27, in these chapters Nephi never acknowledges that a text from Isaiah serves as his framework. The reader is left to discover that through his or her own study.

Because Nephi draws so heavily on and so intricately interprets an Isaianic text in 2 Nephi 26–27, these two chapters are an immensely useful resource for examining how scriptural authors understand the nature of prophecy and scriptural "application." As Nephi—however discreetly—displays his readerly strategies while he works on Isaiah, he makes it possible to recognize the process he has in mind when he speaks of "likening" scripture to oneself, as well as, somewhat more implicitly, what he takes to be the nature of the written scriptural texts to which he addresses himself in study. Because Nephi encourages his readers to liken scripture as he himself does, careful analysis of Nephi's approach to interpreting Isaiah should be of great profit to every reader of the Book of Mormon.

That Nephi feels comfortable weaving his own prophecies into the text of Isaiah is itself a telling thing. That he not only adds his own statements to the Isaianic text but also adjusts the "quoted" scripture freely is still more telling. It appears that Nephi's work of likening implies at least two things about the nature of scripture and its application: (1) The work of likening allows what might otherwise become the "dead letter" of a scriptural text to come back to life. Likening thus appears to be a kind of scriptural resurrection, a way of giving new life to scripture. (2) The work of likening a text may only be able to breathe life into a text through a prophetic editing process in which the text may be adjusted, recontextualized, and intentionally appropriated. It is not entirely inappropriate, therefore, to say that the work of likening can give new life to a scriptural text only by first "killing it." As Paul says concerning resurrection generally: "that which thou sowest is not quickened, except it die" (1 Corinthians 15:36).

Two caveats must be mentioned regarding these two implications.

First, it should be noted that likening a text is, for Nephi, a question of weaving into the scriptural text *not* the banalities of everyday life (an application of the scriptures to everyday life), but rather truths one has learned regarding the meaning and importance of the Abrahamic covenant through some kind of revelatory or prophetic experience. It might thus be said that it is only a *prophet*—though that word must be taken in its broadest definition as referring to anyone who has "the spirit of prophecy" (see 2 Nephi 25:4)—who can authoritatively give new life to a scriptural text. (This first caveat is not meant to discourage the work of likening, but to encourage recognition that likening seems, for Nephi, only to be likening when it is undertaken with the spirit of prophecy.)

Second, it should be recognized that Nephi does not introduce likening into the Isaianic text as a foreign element. Rather, careful reading of scripture reveals that the prophetic texts present *within themselves* a kind of proto-likening or a preliminary "metaphorizing" of what they have to say. In 2 Nephi 26–27 and its appropriation of Isaiah 29, not only does Nephi creatively adapt Isaianic images into new, prophetically projected contexts, but Isaiah *himself* consistently employs images, metaphors, and symbols that *are already open to multiple interpretations and readily available for future adaptation*. Likening scripture is, then, not a way of misappropriating scripture but of giving attention to the multiple (but unrealized) prophetic possibilities already at work in the text.

Nephi's use of the Isaianic image of a "book that is sealed" (Isaiah 29:11) aptly illustrates these points. In Isaiah's original prophecy, this image is clearly presented as a metaphor ("the vision of all is become unto you *as* the words of a book that is sealed") in a two-verse prose excursus in the middle of a longer poetic text. Nephi seems to have picked up on the richness inherent in this image, and he expands much more dramatically on verses 11–12 than on other parts of Isaiah 29. Recognizing that even Isaiah employs the image only as a symbol, Nephi repurposes that symbol to stand for something whose emergence he had witnessed in his own apocalyptic revelation (in 1 Nephi 11–14): the Book of Mormon. He thus weaves his own prophetic anticipations of what modern Latter-day Saints easily recognize as the "Charles Anthon incident" into the text of Isaiah, resurrecting the Isaianic text at the same moment that he, as it were, partially "kills" the text's original intentions.

3. How do these chapters provide a clearer understanding of what Nephi is trying to accomplish in his small plates?

Relatively obvious structural markers break Nephi's two books into four major parts:

1. 1 Nephi 1–18 (the story of the founding of the Lehites)
2. 1 Nephi 19–2 Nephi 5 (the division of the Lehites into Nephites and Lamanites)
3. 2 Nephi 6–30 (prophecies concerning the eventual reconciliation of the Nephites and Lamanites)
4. 2 Nephi 31–33 (concluding thoughts)

Chapters 26–27 of 2 Nephi are thus part of a much larger section of Nephi's record (2 Nephi 6–30) that comprises what Nephi himself described as the "more sacred" part of his writings (1 Nephi 19:5). In fact, these two chapters are part of a six-chapter sequence (2 Nephi 25–30) within that larger section in which Nephi not only joins his brother Jacob in offering commentary on Isaiah (see 2 Nephi 6–10), but also returns to the central apocalyptic vision of his first book, popularly known as the vision of the tree of life (1 Nephi 11–14). This last connection is of particular interpretive significance: it helps to make clear that 2 Nephi 26–27 is to be read not only according to the context provided for it in 2 Nephi, but also according to its thematic connections to the privileged vision of 1 Nephi.

This return to the apocalyptic vision of 1 Nephi 11–14 in 2 Nephi 25–30 emphatically marks the way that Nephi's record privileges the earlier vision. Indeed, it might be taken as a kind of justification for offering a speculative (but reasoned) reconstruction of the stages in which Nephi's record took shape.

Stage 1: First, a number of details might be culled from Nephi's record to suggest that he originally planned only to write what is now 1 Nephi 1–18. This is not only suggested by the obvious textual break between 1 Nephi 18 and 1 Nephi 19 (the latter of which opens with Nephi's detailed description of his textual project), but also by the three earliest descriptions Nephi offers of what he is writing, found in the heading for First Nephi (immediately before 1 Nephi 1), in 1 Nephi 6, and in 1 Nephi 9. These, taken together with 2 Nephi 5:30–33, which appears to report the original commandment Nephi was given concerning the writing of his record, support the possibility that Nephi initially intended only to write a shorter record that detailed the journey from Jerusalem to the New World.

If this position has any merit, it in turn would suggest that Nephi's earliest project in writing the small plates was to use the narrative of the journey from Jerusalem to the New World to foreground and contextualize the visions of Nephi and his father in 1 Nephi 8–15. That is, if Nephi originally intended to write just the first eighteen chapters of First Nephi (and nothing of Second Nephi), then Nephi's small plates were first and foremost a setting forth of the apocalyptic vision of the eventual emergence of the Nephite record, the very theme to which Nephi eventually returns in 2 Nephi 25–30.

Stage 2: Nephi's purposes would seem eventually to have changed, something he attempts to explain in the first verses of 1 Nephi 19 (and the final verses of 2 Nephi 5). In this second understanding of his project, Nephi recasts the whole of his initial project (1 Nephi 1–18) as a kind of prologue to the much more comprehensive story he now intends to tell. After laying out the difficulties that followed after the journey to the New World (in 1 Nephi 19 – 2 Nephi 5), Nephi begins to write what he describes as the actual core of his record, the mandated "plain and precious parts" of "the ministry and the prophecies" (1 Nephi 19: 3). At this point, he apparently understood his record as falling into three major parts—1 Nephi 1–18; 1 Nephi 19 – 2 Nephi 5; and 2 Nephi 6–30—the last section returning to the themes of the first in order to show how the difficulties of the second section might eventually be overcome.

In Nephi's second understanding of his textual project (especially taking 2 Nephi 25–27 as a guide), it seems Nephi understood his purpose to be to create a text that would (1) be retained and carefully read by his people so that it would (2) serve as a kind of impetus or at least inspiration for his people to begin to write the record of which he had prophesied. In essence, he saw his record as a systematic injunction to his people to pay attention to their divine task to compile a record that would eventually serve as the means of salvation for both scattered Israel and the Gentiles.

Stage 3: Finally, at some point, Nephi seems to have decided to add a conclusion to his record (note both the finality of the last verses of 2 Nephi 30 and the hesitation to begin again in the first verses of 2 Nephi 31).

Whatever else might be said about Nephi's concluding words, it is very clear that they are charcterized by an important advance in Nephi's understanding of the purpose of his small plates record. Whereas he earlier understood his record first as a contextualized prophecy of the writing and eventual emergence of the Nephite record and second as a kind of systematic injunction to the Nephites to write and then to bury that Nephite record, he seems in his last words to have recognized that he was, in the small plates themselves, writing part of that record. The key passage is 2 Nephi 33: 13, in which Nephi adopts the crucial language of Isaiah 29—which forms the backbone of his earlier understanding in 2 Nephi 25–30—in order to identify his own record with the one whose emergence in the last days he has announced. At long last, it appears Nephi realized that he had already begun to construct the record that would be central to the unfolding of God's plan for history in the last days.

In the end, chapters 26–27 of 2 Nephi provide an essential background against which Nephi's ultimate understanding of the role of the small plates as an integral part of the latter-day record emerges. As Nephi works through Isaiah 29, he comes to grasp prophetically the necessity of such a record, and in doing so, it can be argued, he initiates the thoughts and prayers that will eventually lead him to a reconsideration of his own record's future role.

4. What does 2 Nephi 26–27 teach us about the nature, role, and place of the Book of Mormon?

One of the first things that ought to strike the reader of the Book of Mormon is its profound self-awareness. The Book of Mormon repeatedly prophesies of itself (see 1 Nephi 13: 25, 35; 3 Nephi 21:1–7; 25: 21–22; 26: 8–10; Mormon 5: 12; Moroni 10:3–4), and its own authors consciously proclaim its weakness (see 1 Nephi 13:39; 2 Nephi 29: 10–11; Ether 12: 23–25). It should come as no surprise, then, that a crucial part of the Book of Mormon's prophetic self-awareness involves an explication of its own role in the latter-day fulfillment of what might be called the "Lehitic covenant."

The Lehitic covenant consists of four basic elements:

1. A promised land is given to the children of Lehi (2 Nephi 1:5).
2. Prosperity in the land is predicated on obedience to the commandments (Jarom 1:9).
3. Lehi's seed will never perish (2 Nephi 25:21).
4. A record will bring Lehi's seed to a knowledge of their covenant (Enos 1:13, 16; Ether 4:17).

While the Book of Mormon makes frequent reference to each element, consistent theological attention is paid to the fourth element in particular. As early as the title page one finds the announcement that the writings of Nephi and his descendants will eventually be taken "to the Lamanites, . . . that they may know the covenants of the Lord." Nephi is by far the most theologically interested Book of Mormon writer on this point. He further informs readers of the book that it "shall come forth, and . . . there shall be many [among the Gentiles] which shall believe the words . . . and they shall carry them forth unto the remnant of our seed" (2 Nephi 30:3).

Nephi's writings most directly manifest this awareness of the Book of Mormon's latter-day emergence in the incorporation of Isaianic prophecy found in 2 Nephi 26–27: "The Lord God shall bring forth unto you the words of a book, and they shall be the words of them which have slumbered" (2 Nephi 27:6). Accordingly, these two chapters proceed to outline the purpose, composition, and emergence of the Book of Mormon in striking detail.

In 2 Nephi 26–27, Nephi prophesies of two destructions and their relationship to the future record. The first destruction is that of the Nephites (2 Nephi 26:4–6, 9–11) and the second is that of the Gentiles in the latter days (2 Nephi 27:2). For Nephi, these destructions are inseparably linked by his concern for the prophesied record: the Nephite destruction necessitates the *writing* of the record (2 Nephi 26:17), while the Gentile destruction calls for its *emergence* (2 Nephi 27:6). Interspersed among the various parts of this broad outline in 2 Nephi 26–27 are references to the prayers of the fathers (2 Nephi 26:15), warnings regarding the obstacles to covenant fulfillment (secret combinations, for example; see 2 Nephi 26:22; 2 Nephi 27:27), and a detailed prophecy about the unlearned man to whom the sealed record is given (2 Nephi 27:15–26).

Above and beyond simply announcing the record's *relationship* to the covenant, 2 Nephi 26–27 outlines the actual *mechanics* of the covenant's fulfillment. In the very center of the prophecy, sandwiched between the two separate destructions and their concern with the one record, we find the following statement: "the Lord . . . denieth none that come unto him, black and white, bond and free, male and female; and he remembereth the heathen; and all are alike unto God, both Jew and Gentile" (2 Nephi 27:33; see also vv. 24–28). Nephi here sets up a series of polar opposites, each one a political distinction imposed by the world, in order to demonstrate the gospel's essential indifference to worldly categorization. Nephi sees the latter-day world as politically structured in particular by the question of Jew and Gentile (2 Nephi 27:1).

This errant gospel, announced via the Book of Mormon, attempts to distract the Jewish-Gentile polemic by creating a genuinely generic kingdom: the house of Israel. Indeed, the title page makes this particularly clear by announcing its intention to convince *both* "Jew and Gentile that JESUS is the CHRIST," while still maintaining the entirely separate category of "the House of Israel."

In light of these details, one might argue that 2 Nephi 26–27 provides the most comprehensive and detailed self-analysis in the Book of Mormon. Despite the fact that there are *two* destructions in question, for Nephi, there remains only *one* record. He builds on this intimation of unity to ensure that readers understand that the work of the gospel will outstrip categorization. These chapters prophesy of the role of the record across both temporal (old world vs. latter-day) and ethnic (Jew vs. Gentile) gaps, declaring its intention to distract the artificial divisions between peoples and generations into the working out of a unified covenant.

Nephi, Isaiah, and Europe

Joseph M. Spencer

DETAILS SUGGEST that 2 NEPHI 6–30 is somehow "*more* sacred" than everything else in Nephi's record.[1] Following these indications, Elder Jeffrey R. Holland says: "One could argue convincingly that the primary purpose for recording, preserving, and then translating the small plates of Nephi was to bring forth to the dispensation of the fulness of times the testimony" of Nephi, Jacob, and Isaiah contained specifically in those twenty-five chapters. Indeed, Elder Holland goes on to describe these three prophets as "standing like sentinels at the gate of the [Book of Mormon]," where they serve to "admit us into the scriptural presence of the Lord."[2]

Admitting the centrality of 2 Nephi 6–30 to Nephi's overarching textual purposes, we must further recognize the structurally privileged role given to one of Nephi's three "sentinels" in particular. Nephi structurally presents himself and his brother Jacob as parallel popularizers and expositors of Isaiah. Not only are the thirteen so-called Isaiah chapters (2 Nephi 11–24) positioned between Jacob's (2 Nephi 6–10) and Nephi's (2 Nephi 25–30) teachings, but both Jacob's and Nephi's contributions are built on quotations of and commentaries on still

1. See 1 Nephi 9:3; 19:3–6; 2 Nephi 5:30–33; 11:1–3; 30:18; 31:1. See also Frederick W. Axelgard, "1 and 2 Nephi: An Inspiring Whole," *BYU Studies* 26/4 (Fall 1986): 53–66.

2. Jeffrey R. Holland, *Christ and the New Covenant* (Salt Lake City: Deseret Book, 1997), 35–36.

other chapters from Isaiah. Isaiah is, in a word, the honored keynote speaker of the small plates, the figure around whose schedule everything else is organized.

Consequently, given that the aim of the small plates was to exhibit the shape of the early Nephite ministry,[3] we only come to grips with the record when we begin to ask how Nephi read and likened Isaiah.[4] Here, then, I would like to address the following question: *Why Isaiah?* What did Nephi see in Isaiah that so impressed him? In my response to this question, I will privilege 2 Nephi 26–27, obviously because that is the focus of the present volume, but also because it is there more than anywhere else that Nephi's interpretive approach to Isaiah is on display. I first consider these chapters while ignoring their Isaianic content, considering only their theological claims. Having thus derived an idea of Nephi's predominant theological concerns, I then address the question of what motivated Nephi's interest in Isaiah.

Nephi without Isaiah

Second Nephi 26–27 speaks of two quite specifically delineated historical periods. The first, described in 2 Nephi 26:1–18, stretches from the visit of Jesus Christ to the Lehites to the final destruction of the Nephites—roughly the period described in the historical books of 3 Nephi, 4 Nephi, and Mormon. The second, taken up at greater length in 2 Nephi 26:19–27:35, begins with the modern arrival of the Old World Gentiles among the dwindling New World Lamanites.[5] Though these

3. See 1 Nephi 9:3–4; 10:1; 19:3–6.

4. I distinguish here between the early Nephite ministry—associated with the small plates—and the later Nephite ministry, associated with the books of Mosiah, Alma, and Helaman. Both Isaiah and Nephi's covenantal concerns disappear from the later ministry, something that seems to have been a consequence of Abinadi's entanglement with King Noah. See Joseph M. Spencer, *An Other Testament: On Typology* (Salem, OR: Salt Press, 2011); or, more summarily, Joseph M. Spencer, "Prolegomena to Any Future Study of Isaiah in the Book of Mormon," *Claremont Journal of Mormon Studies* 1/1 (April 2011): 53–69.

5. Note that 2 Nephi 25 describes a third period preceding the two discussed in 2 Nephi 26–27—namely, the period from Nephi's own day down to the visit of Christ

two periods are obviously distinct—a full millennium passes after the end of the Nephites and before the Gentile arrival in the New World—they are, according to Nephi, closely connected. On the one hand, Nephi signals an intimate tie between the first period's end and the second period's beginning by using parallel language to describe first the Lamanite destruction of the Nephites and then the Gentile destruction of the Lamanites (2 Nephi 26:18–19). On the other hand, Nephi marks as the definitive event of the second period the sudden appearance of a book written and sealed up in the first period (2 Nephi 26:17; 27:6).

In the end, this complex double relationship between the two historical periods—the one bringing the other to its definitive (obliterative!) end, the other supplementing the one by leaving a book behind—is Nephi's most pressing theological concern in 2 Nephi 26–27. Because it is most richly articulated, I believe, in 2 Nephi 26:33–27:6, I will focus the rest of my analysis on those verses in particular.

2 Nephi 26:33

The last verse of 2 Nephi 26 draws to its close a fourteen-verse tangent describing and polemicizing against the wickedness of the Old World Gentiles after they arrive among the New World Lamanites (2 Nephi 26:20–33). Helpfully, this last verse summarizes the conclusions Nephi draws from his aside. After asserting that "none of these [Gentile] iniquities come of the Lord; for he doeth that which is good among the children of men; and he doeth nothing save it be plain unto the children of men," Nephi announces the rigorous *universality* of the gospel: "and he inviteth them *all* to come unto him and partake of his goodness; and he denieth *none* that come unto him, black *and* white, bond *and* free, male *and* female; and he remembereth the heathen; and *all* are alike unto God, *both* Jew *and* Gentile" (2 Nephi 26:33, emphases added).

Nephi here echoes Paul's declaration in Galatians 3:28 that in Christ there is "neither Jew nor Greek, . . . neither bond nor free, . . .

---

in 3 Nephi—and that 2 Nephi 28–30 continues to discuss the second of the two periods discussed in 2 Nephi 26–27.

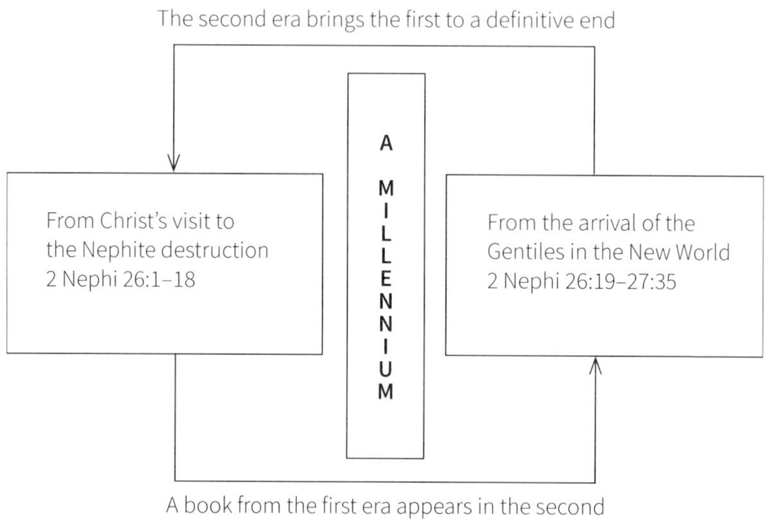

Figure 1

neither male nor female."[6] On the grounds of this allusion (of sorts), it seems Nephi shares with Paul what French philosopher Alain Badiou calls Paul's kerygma of "universalism," an approach to preaching that "refuses to stigmatize differences and customs"—whether economic (bond/free), racial (black/white), or even sexual (male/female). Such universalism, as Badiou further explains, amounts to neither an affirmation nor a celebration of differences, but rather to "an *in*difference that tolerates differences" because they are, in the end, essentially immaterial. That is, Pauline universalism "accommodates" such differences and customs only "so that the process of their subjective *disqualification* might pass through them," over the course of what Latter-day Saints call the process of conversion.[7]

6. Wayne Meeks points out the likelihood that this Pauline formulation actually has its roots in the ancient Christian baptismal liturgy. Compare 1 Corinthians 12:13 and Colossians 3:11. Wayne A. Meeks, ed., *The Writings of St. Paul* (New York: Norton, 1972), 18.

7. Alain Badiou, *Saint Paul: The Foundation of Universalism*, trans. Ray Brassier (Stanford: Stanford University Press, 2003), 99, emphases added. Some have, of course, criticized Badiou's interpretation of Pauline universalism, as in, for instance, John D. Caputo and Linda Martín Alcoff, eds., *St. Paul among the Philosophers* (Bloomington

As can be seen when 2 Nephi 26:33 and Galatians 3:28 are brought together, this universalism works on a logic that can be described on the one hand as a logic of the "neither/nor," or on the other hand as a logic of the "both/and." Genuinely universal truth as such privileges *neither* the one *nor* the other, or—what amounts to the same thing—equally privileges *both* the one *and* the other. But what does this logic imply, whether in the negative shape of the "neither/nor" or the positive shape of the "both/and"? At least the following:

1. Normal ("fallen") situations are characterized by the differential relationship between two binarily opposed categories, each dependent on (the dismissal of) the other for its identity. The one is *not the other*; the other is *not the one*.
2. Truth, though, however it ultimately traverses a situation, is effectively indifferent to the differences that establish the identities of the categories making up the situation. The truth regards *neither* the one *nor* the other; the truth addresses itself *both* to the one *and* to the other.

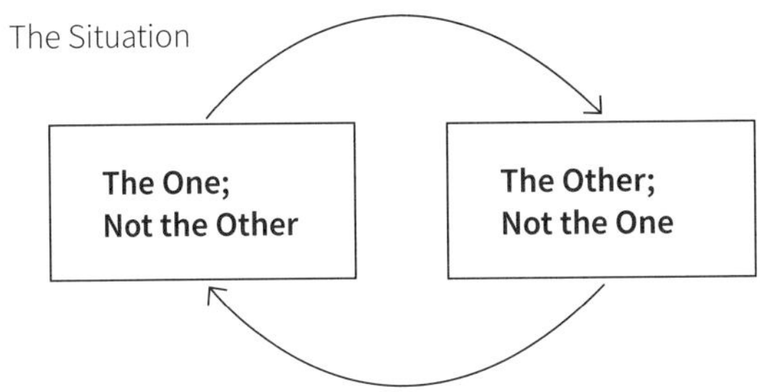

Figure 2

and Indianapolis: Indiana University Press, 2009). Critics generally point out that Badiou's privileging of the neither/nor of Galatians 3:28 would ultimately *cancel* all diversity in the construction of a vague commonality. I believe, though, that this criticism misses Badiou's point. To speak of the disqualification of differences is not to call for their obliteration, but to suggest that precisely because universal truths are universal, they refuse to allow economic, racial, sexual, or other cultural distinctions to be what ultimately qualifies an individual. For Badiou's Paul, what qualifies the individual is faith in, hope in light of, and charity with regard to the revelatory event. In the words of Doctrine and Covenants 4:5, "faith, hope, [and] charity . . . qualify him for the work."

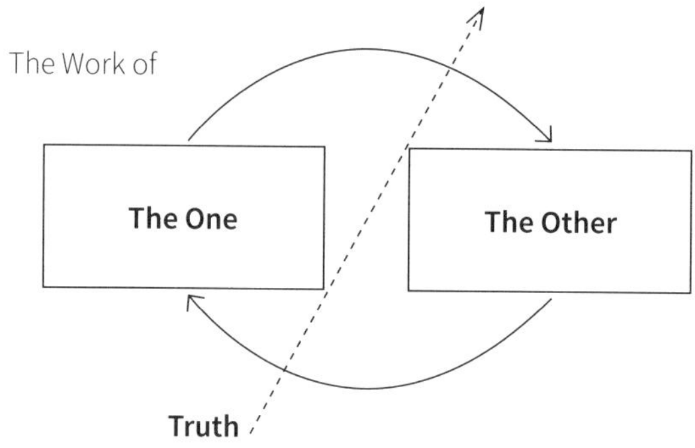

Figure 3

In terms of 2 Nephi 26:33, then, the truth of the gospel—to which God "inviteth . . . all" and from which God "denieth none"—distracts attention from the "two components of the articulated whole," from the two poles of the polarized situation that are inevitably "in a relation of reciprocal maintenance and mirroring."[8] One could say that the truth distracts polarity *itself*—distracts it, as Jean-Luc Marion says commenting on another Pauline passage, "as a magnet distracts a compass, in depriving it of all reference to a fixed pole."[9] And Nephi provides a list of three such polarities distracted by the announcement of the gospel: "black and white, bond and free, male and female." But in the end, Nephi privileges none of these politically crucial and morally complex polarities, focusing instead with what is apparently for him the most important polarity-to-be-distracted of all: the neither/nor or both/and of "*Jew and Gentile.*"

The particular weight Nephi gives to *this* polarity is twice marked in the text. First, Nephi separates the privileged polarity from the others by inserting between them an emphatic reiteration of the universality of faithful preaching ("he inviteth them all to come unto him and partake of his goodness; and he denieth none that come unto him [first iteration of universality], black and white, bond and free, male

8. Badiou, *Saint Paul,* 13.

9. Jean-Luc Marion, *God without Being,* trans. Thomas A. Carlson (Chicago: University of Chicago Press, 1991), 90.

and female [list of "lesser" polarities]; and he remembereth the heathen; and all are alike unto God [second iteration of universality], both Jew and Gentile [identification of "greater" polarity]"). Second, though, and more important, Nephi dedicates the whole of his next chapter (2 Nephi 27) to outlining the disqualification of the polarized relationship between the Jews and the Gentiles—and he does so without mentioning racial, economic, or sexual politics. For Nephi, it seems, the resources of the gospel can and should be put not only (and not even primarily!) to the task of dismantling racism, economic disparity, and sexism, but also (and more consistently and more dedicatedly!) to the infinitely more demanding task of dismantling the problematic relationship between Jews and Gentiles.

2 Nephi 27:1–6

Given Nephi's focus, in 2 Nephi 27, on the Jewish/Gentile problem, I will turn there next, focusing on the first six verses. Two questions, drawn from the above reading of 2 Nephi 26:33, will guide my interpretation. First, what *is* the relationship between the Jews and the Gentiles? Second, *how* is that relationship to be dismantled by the truth of the gospel?

2 Nephi 27:1: "But, behold, in the last days, or in the days of the Gentiles—yea, behold all the nations of the Gentiles and also the Jews, both those who shall come upon this land and those who shall be upon other lands, yea, even upon all the lands of the earth, behold, they will be drunken with iniquity and all manner of abominations." This verse calls for four remarks. (1) Despite the hand-wringing that sometimes appears in print over this question, the historical identities of both the Gentiles and the Jews are clear in the text: Nephi consistently identifies the Jews as those displaced from Jerusalem by the Babylonian exile,[10] and the Gentiles are—in light especially of the vision in 1 Nephi 11–14—understood to be the nations specifically of Europe.[11]

---

10. Cf. 1 Nephi 2:13; 10:4; 2 Nephi 25:5–6; 30:4; 33:8.

11. Thus Brant Gardner, commenting on 1 Nephi 13:1–3, even as he points out other interpretive possibilities, notes: "The modern reader can easily interpret this passage as [referring to] the Europeans, separated from America by the Atlantic Ocean."

(2) Though Nephi usually distinguishes Gentiles and Jews sharply (the former consisting of so many settled "nations" or "kingdoms" and the latter consisting instead of a wandering people, cut off from their land), here Nephi lumps them together as "all the nations of the Gentiles and also the Jews." (3) Whatever its beginnings or its historical trajectory, Nephi here prophesies that the relationship between the Jews and Gentiles will come to be of undeniable global importance in the last days: "all the nations of the Gentiles and also the Jews" include not only "this land," but also "other lands," indeed, "all the lands of the earth." (4) Nephi implies that the global spread of the tensions underlying the Jewish/Gentile entanglement cannot be disconnected from the latter-day saturation of the world with "iniquity and all manner of abominations."

Bringing the first three points together, one could say that Nephi accurately predicts what Jacques Derrida has called our "globalatinized" world—a still thoroughly Roman world not quite so post-colonial as it professes itself to be, saturated by European culture and concerns, and particularly by that European (and strictly European!) question of the meaning of Judaism (or of the larger Judeo-Christian tradition).[12] But Nephi goes further with his fourth point, speaking of a world given as much to "iniquity and all manner of abominations" as to the so-called Jewish question. And indeed, Nephi goes on in the next four verses (2 Nephi 27:2–5) to describe the polarized Jewish/Gentile world of the last days as speeding unchecked toward destruction. The polarized European world Nephi had seen in vision will, he predicts, be "visited of the Lord of Hosts, with thunder and with earthquake, and with a great noise, and with storm, and with tempest, and with the flame of devouring fire" (2 Nephi 27:2). And all this will come, according to Nephi, because those of whom he speaks—Jew and Gentile alike—will have "closed [their] eyes" and "rejected the prophets" (2 Nephi 27:5).

Brant A. Gardner, *Second Witness: Analytical and Contextual Commentary on the Book of Mormon*, 6 vols. (Salt Lake City: Greg Kofford Books, 2007), 1:228.

12. Jacques Derrida, "Faith and Knowledge: The Two Sources of 'Religion' at the Limits of Reason Alone," trans. Samuel Weber, in *Religion*, ed. Jacques Derrida and Gianni Vattimo (Stanford: Stanford University Press, 1998), 1–78.

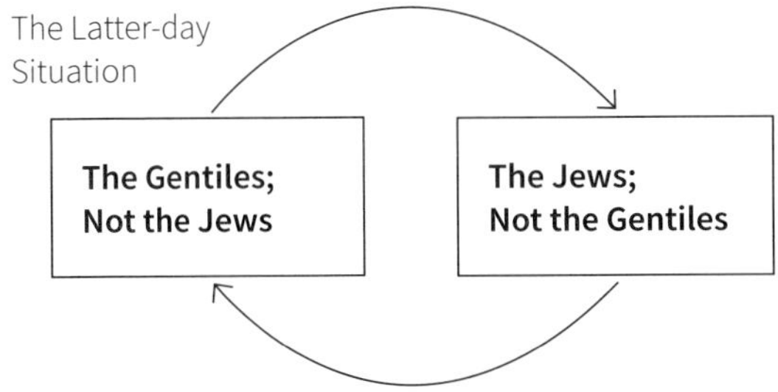

Figure 4

As if to help the reader make sense of this situation, Nephi draws in these same four verses on at least four (Isaianic) images to describe the *incapacitated* state of the Jewish/Gentile world of the last days: the dreamer, the drunk, the sleeper, and the willfully blind. The common thread running through all four images is the idea that each imagined figure exercises a desire to avoid reality. The dreamer, the drunk, the sleeper, and the willfully blind *all* avoid reality by submitting to some kind of ideological or idolatrous fantasy. And history makes clear how central avoidance and ideology have been to the European entanglement between Jews and Gentiles. On the one hand, Gentiles persecute or often enough attempt to obliterate the Jews in order to totally maintain their own thoroughly ideological identity, only the most spectacular instance being the Teutonic "blood and soil" ideology and its aftermath in the camps of Nazi Germany. On the other hand, Jews have just as often assumed a nationalist ideology of radical exception, even at times borrowing the terms of their self-definition from Nazi ideology. Thus, to quote Badiou again, "Jewish discourse and [Gentile] discourse are the two aspects of the *same* figure of mastery."[13]

But if it is their idolatrous obsession with each other that blinds, inebriates, lulls, and sets to dreaming the latter-day Gentiles and Jews, it remains to be decided what it is that—*in* their blindness, drunkenness, slumber, and dreams—the Jews and Gentiles fail to see. What is it that, according to Nephi, the Gentiles and Jews of the last days "close

13. Badiou, *Saint Paul,* 42, emphasis added. See also Alain Badiou, *Polemics,* trans. Steve Corcoran (New York: Verso, 2006), 155–254.

[their] eyes" *to*? What is that *truth*—void of their shared situation—that neither Jew nor Gentile notices because of its effective *in*difference to the differences they desperately labor to establish, to affirm, even, all too often nowadays, to celebrate? What, in a word, is the truth that the totalized world of the thoroughly European last days, as much in ecumenism as in contention, obscures—the truth that would, in Joseph Smith's words, "revolutionize the whole world"?[14]

Whatever the content of that truth, Nephi is clear about the manner of its revelation: "And it shall come to pass that the Lord God shall bring forth unto you *the words of a book,* and they shall be the words of them which have slumbered" (2 Nephi 27:6, emphasis added). The truth's appearance is accomplished by the sudden emergence of a book that—precisely because it comes from a definitively voided ancient people, completely lost to history—necessarily registers as an unanticipated and essentially inessential supplement to the situation in which it emerges. But the very inessentiality of the book—its irreversible weakness—is precisely its strength, ensuring that it is as much for the Jews as for the Gentiles, as much for the Gentiles as for the Jews. Indeed, because the book concerns itself with a truth that, in its universalism, distracts the polarized global politics surrounding European Jewry, it is this book alone, according to Nephi, that will give *a name* to what the Jewish/Gentile hegemony has voided in its global dominance: the *remnant* (of Israel).[15]

The book of the remnant, naturally, is the Book of Mormon. According to its title page, the Book of Mormon is meant to convince both "Jew and Gentile that Jesus is the Christ" *only while it goes about*

---

14. Joseph Smith Jr., *The Words of Joseph Smith: The Contemporary Accounts of the Nauvoo Discourses of the Prophet Joseph,* ed. Andrew F. Ehat and Lyndon W. Cook (Provo, UT: Religious Studies Center, Brigham Young University, 1980), 367.

15. With his focus on the remnant, Nephi is again in line with Saint Paul. See the remarkable discussion of Pauline remnant theology—coupled with an important corrective to Badiou's understanding of Pauline universalism—in Giorgio Agamben, *The Time That Remains: A Commentary on the Letter to the Romans,* trans. Patricia Dailey (Stanford: Stanford University Press, 2005), 44–58. See also Giorgio Agamben, *Remnants of Auschwitz: The Witness and the Archive,* trans. Daniel Heller-Roazen (New York: Zone Books, 2002).

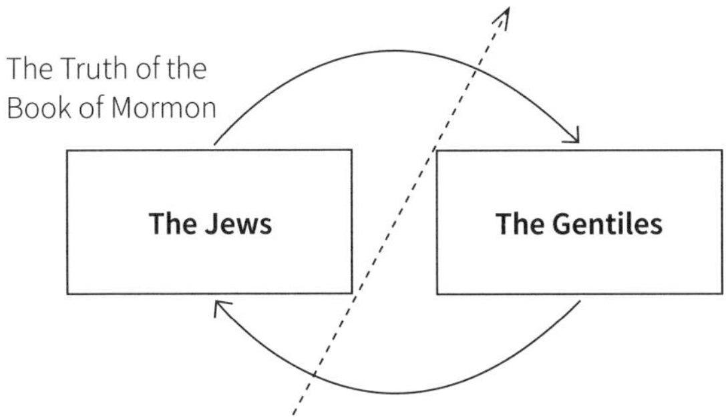

Figure 5

its more fundamental work of addressing the voided "remnant of the House of Israel," which has not, despite appearances, been "cast off forever" from the "covenants of the Lord."[16] And according to Nephi, the Book of Mormon aims to reveal that the void of the Jewish/Gentile situation today called "Europe" is the remnant of Israel—indeed, that *both* Jews *and* Gentiles have misinterpreted scripture by "tak[ing] away from the gospel of the Lamb many parts which are plain and most precious," particularly the "covenants of the Lord" made to *all* Israel (1 Nephi 13:26).

This truth, the universal truth of the Abrahamic covenant announced by the Book of Mormon, is one that could—or has indeed already begun to—"revolutionize the whole world."[17] As Richard Bushman says: "The Book of Mormon," and Nephi in particular, "works out

16. The title page mentions convincing Jews and Gentiles only *after* ("and also") its intentions concerning the remnant. It thus appears that the more generically Christian project of the Book of Mormon is something like a by-product of its more specifically Israelite project.

17. Harold Bloom, interestingly, opened his study of Mormonism with an excerpt from Kierkegaard's journal: "Even now, in 1848, it certainly looks as though politics were everything; but it will be seen that the catastrophe (the Revolution) corresponds to us and is the obverse of the Reformation: then everything pointed to a religious movement and proved to be political; now everything points to a political movement, but will become religious." Harold Bloom, *The American Religion: The Emergence of the Post-Christian Nation* (New York: Simon & Schuster, 1992), 13. That Nephi places such heavy emphasis on the role of Europe in the story he has to tell deserves more attention. In one sense, 1 Nephi 11–14 sets up Mormonism itself as the true heir of the American

[a] schema of world history down to the brass-tack details," calling for a "recovery of the entire experience of all the world's peoples through the translation and absorption [into this schema] of their histories."[18] In deference to the Book of Mormon emphasis on the reconstructed *remnant* of Israel, one must understand this translation/absorption to take the shape of adoption into the generic family of Abraham.[19] And thus it seems that the Nauvoo project of sealing into one enormous covenant family every single person who has dwelt on the earth, *whether Jew or Gentile,* is firmly rooted in the Book of Mormon as Nephi envisioned and inaugurated it.

Obviously, much more can—and needs to be—said about these themes. My purpose here, though, is only to get a basic sense of Nephi's theological interests in order to come back to the larger question of what interested Nephi about Isaiah's writings. For now, then, I will only summarize what I have here discovered in 2 Nephi 26:33–27:6 before turning to my original question.

1. Nephi sees in vision a latter-day world dominated by a polarized European politics of Jewish/Gentile conflict.
2. Nephi sees this conflict eventually disrupted by the appearance and promulgations of a long-since sealed book neither written by nor addressed to the Jews or the Gentiles.
3. Nephi sees this book allowing for the construction of a generic community ("the remnant"), which, made up of *both* Jews *and* Gentiles, is ultimately *neither* a Gentile *nor* a Jewish nation.

Revolution, and that precisely inasmuch as it maintains fidelity to the Book of Mormon with its emphasis on Israel's covenant.

18. Richard Lyman Bushman, "The Book of Mormon in Early Mormon History," in Richard Lyman Bushman, *Believing History: Latter-day Saint Essays,* ed. Reid L. Neilson and Jed Woodworth (New York: Columbia University Press, 2004), 74, 76.

19. It is absolutely crucial to insist that the horizon of the Abrahamic covenant is the *remnant* of Israel, and not Israel *pure and simple.* Scripture consistently draws a rigorous distinction between the family *to be constructed* and the family *naturally produced.* Unfortunately, the few available systematic readings of the Abrahamic covenant in the Book of Mormon are generally marred by a failure to maintain this distinction with full rigor.

Nephi with Isaiah

What did Nephi see in Isaiah, given his theological concerns? That is, why does Nephi not only exposit the themes analyzed above, but also weave them into, couple them with, and use them to expound—indeed, *to liken*—the writings of Isaiah?

Certainly, there is profound continuity between Nephi and Isaiah in their interest in the Jewish/Gentile relationship. Isaiah is, as the standard commentaries make clear, quite as concerned as Nephi about constructing a kingdom as open to the Gentiles as to the Jews, and as open to the Jews as to the Gentiles.[20] While Isaiah's interest in this question seems to have arisen from his being witness to the collapse of the northern kingdom of Israel, Nephi's arguably arose from his being witness in turn to the collapse of the southern kingdom of Judah. But whatever their individual motivations, both prophets are closely attuned to the relationship between the "chosen" people and "all the other" nations making up the world.

Isaiah, moreover, shares with Nephi the idea that a generic or universal *remnant* will be what eventually distracts the Jewish/Gentile polarity that dissimulates the significance of the Abrahamic covenant. Indeed, it is almost certain that Nephi drew his remnant theology directly from Isaiah's writings. Certainly, Isaiah—along with Micah, whose sayings about the remnant significantly appear in 3 Nephi—is *the* source for any biblically rooted remnant theology.[21] Of course, Isaiah did not *invent* remnant theology, but there is no question about his having been its most innovative *systematizer*.[22] At any rate, however much of his remnant theology Nephi borrowed from Isaiah, it is clear why he was interested in his Old World predecessor's writings.

---

20. Note that, like Nephi, Isaiah privileges this particular polarized problematic above others—most notably over the problems of economic disparity (the polarized relationship between rich and poor), which nonetheless plays a substantial role in his writings.

21. Note, for example, that Paul drew on many of the same Isaiah texts as Nephi, something that likely explains, in part, the theological similarities between Nephi and Paul.

22. See Gerhard F. Hasel, *The Remnant: The History and Theology of the Remnant Idea from Genesis to Isaiah* (Berrien Springs, MI: Andrews University Press, 1972).

What undoubtedly clinched Nephi's fascination with Isaiah, however, was the latter's consistent concern with written, sealed, buried, and only eventually circulated texts, most helpfully exposited by Gerhard von Rad.[23] Indeed, in terms of his interest in the Jewish/Gentile polarity and the role of the remnant in distracting that polarity, Isaiah differs from other Old World prophets only in that he was more prolific and more systematic (and perhaps a more compelling poet). But Isaiah is more or less alone among the Hebrew prophets for his interest in writing. For Isaiah alone, the construction of the remnant would be effected through the eschatological emergence of a *written text.* And the precision with which Nephi reads Isaiah's complex organization of this theme (brilliantly exposited by Edgar Conrad) is, frankly, startling.[24] What drew Nephi's attention above all else, it seems, was thus Isaiah's heavy emphasis on the written word.

But what turned Nephi's attention particularly to these themes in the first place—to these themes that *eventually* attracted him to the writings of Isaiah? That is, what focused Nephi on sealed texts, and on the latent universalism of the Abrahamic covenant? Simply put, Nephi's theological interests—made so clear in 2 Nephi 26–27—all derived from his apocalyptic desert vision, recorded in 1 Nephi 11–14. There, camped a short distance from Jerusalem and with almost his whole life still ahead of him, Nephi saw in vision everything that drove his theological interests: the coming and death of the Messiah, the usurpation of those events by the "great and abominable" Gentile church, the decimation of the New World "branch" of Israel, the eventual contact between Europe and the Americas, the subsequent translation and promulgation of a sealed book, and the construction and exaltation of the remnant. In the end, what focused Nephi from first to last on Isaiah seems to have been the consonance between this vision and the basic concerns of Isaiah's writings.

---

23. See Gerhard von Rad, *Old Testament Theology,* 2 vols., trans. D. M. G. Stalker (New York: Harper & Row, 1965), 2:147–69.

24. See Edgar W. Conrad, *Reading Isaiah* (Minneapolis: Fortress Press, 1991). On Nephi's careful employment of Isaiah's "theology of writing," see Spencer, *An Other Testament.*

But, interestingly, it is also in terms of this same vision that the starkest point of disparity between Nephi and Isaiah can be detected. While Isaiah understands the Gentiles broadly as all the nations of the world, Nephi uses the term to refer specifically to European nations. Of course, the reasons for this difference are not hard to guess. First and foremost, it seems to be a question of the startling *specificity* of Nephi's apocalyptic vision. He had seen in vision not only *that* the Old World covenants would eventually come to the attention of the New World Lamanites, but also *how* that would happen. And because he saw that as happening *only* through the Bible's geographical crossing of the European Continent and historical traversal of the European Middle Ages, Nephi uniquely emphasized the curious role of Europe in the unfolding of Isaiah's vision of world history—a role of which Isaiah himself apparently knew nothing.

There is, then, at least one important point of tension between Isaiah's writings *themselves* and Isaiah's writings *as Nephi employs them.* Though both Nephi and Isaiah focused on the Jewish/Gentile question, on the construction of the remnant, and on the eschatological role of the written text, these shared themes seem to have had drastically different *settings* for the two prophets. What Isaiah seems only to have anticipated being a local (though still international) series of events, Nephi recognized as a series of global events of universal import.

Importantly, Nephi actually recognizes this tension between his creative use of Isaiah and Isaiah's writings in themselves. He himself marks this tension consistently in his texts by his use of the—all-too-often oversimplified and misappropriated—term *liken.* For Nephi, to liken Isaiah is, at once, (1) to recognize that the texts to be likened have their setting in a completely distinct time and place, (2) nonetheless to see in those texts patterns according to which the covenant always and everywhere functions, and (3) therefore to take those texts as providing a kind of template for making sense of what one has oneself already understood—in Nephi's case, through apocalyptic vision!—of the history of the covenant.[25] For Nephi, in a word, Isaiah is a kind of proto-Nephite

25. It should be noted that this way of interpreting Isaiah is not, according to Nephi, *typological.* One can argue—and I have done so in *An Other Testament*—that

prophet, an Old World figure who—because he focused on the relation between the latent universalism of the Abrahamic covenant and the prophetic task of writing, sealing, recovering, and translating texts—deserves consistent and close Nephite attention.

I suspect that Nephi is to Joseph Smith as Isaiah is to Nephi—that if Isaiah can be taken as a kind of proto-Nephite prophet, Nephi can be taken as a proto-LDS prophet, a prophet whose creative engagement with the theme of writing and its relation to covenant can be put to work productively in attempting to make sense of what the Doctrine and Covenants says about the role of writing in our own dispensation—of the book of the law of God (see D&C 85:5), of writing and rewriting the law by "not[ing it] with a pen" (see D&C 43:8), of the sacerdotal authority to write on earth to have something written in heaven (see D&C 128:9), of the difference between spoken and written scripture (see D&C 68:4), of gifts of translating "*the* book" (see D&C 5:4), of writing by commandment versus writing by wisdom (see D&C 28:5), of the "Lamb's Book of Life" (see D&C 132:19), of writing and keeping a "regular history" (see D&C 47:1), of a written "book of Enoch" originally inscribed "by the finger of inspiration" (see D&C 107:57; Moses 6:5), and so on.[26] In short, I wonder what we might find if we were today to liken Nephi as Nephi likened Isaiah, to recognize in the Book of Mormon so many traces of ideas highlighted in scriptures given in our own dispensation.

In the meanwhile, I believe the reasons for Nephi's investment in Isaiah are clear. And I hope that it has likewise become clear that where we ignore Isaiah in Nephi's writings, we are likely to misunderstand Nephi himself—to miss what Nephi takes to be his most central message and intention. Certainly, much of the task of reading Nephi remains still before us.

Nephi distinguishes between likening and typological interpretation, though Abinadi reorganizes such distinctions later in Nephite history.

26. Several of these texts read differently now than they did in the original. In particular, see Book of Commandments 45:8 for the earlier version of D&C 43:8; Book of Commandments 4:2 for the earlier version of D&C 5:4; and Scott H. Faulring, Kent P. Jackson, and Robert J. Matthews, eds., *Joseph Smith's New Translation of the Bible: Original Manuscripts* (Provo, UT: Religious Studies Center, Brigham Young University, 2004), 97, for the earlier version of Moses 6:5.

How Nephi Shapes His Readers' Perceptions of Isaiah

Heather Hardy and Grant Hardy

We spent our time during this seminar not only thinking about Nephi's use of the prophecies of Isaiah, but also listening to our eleven-year-old son work his way through Mozart's variations on "Ah! vous dirai-je, Maman." It is hard to say which task has been the more challenging, especially given that this charming French title is attached to the rather tedious melody of "Twinkle, Twinkle Little Star." Mozart, of course, does not disappoint. In his twelve variations on this very well known theme, he is inevitably clever, engaging, and joyful. But after several weeks of practice, we readily agreed with Elliot's piano teacher that polishing just six variations would probably be sufficient. At any rate, somewhere in the flow of days, it occurred to us that Mozart's compositional project might, in fact, have something to tell us about Nephi's.

On the next page is the opening of Mozart's "Twinkle" piece (fig. 1). Even someone unable to read music can see the clear delineation of the initial theme and its first variation. Note that the bass line in the variation begins as an exact replica of the bass line in the initial theme—a quotation, if you will. The melody line has a lot of added notes, but if one looks carefully (it starts out as the second note in each of the sixteenth-note clusters) he or she can also see the persistence of the original tune within Mozart's adaptation. He plays a bit with both

Figure 1. Mozart's first variation on the French folk song "Ah! vous dirai-je, Maman."

rhythm and key—note the occasional syncopation and accidentals—but the theme remains recognizable throughout.

Isaiah's prophecies also have a theme, at least in those passages Nephi includes in his own composition. Nephi identifies his understanding of this theme when he tells us that, in response to queries from Laman and Lemuel regarding their father's prophecies, he rehearsed the words of Isaiah as an explanation because Isaiah, too, had spoken "concerning the restoration of the house of Israel" (1 Nephi 15:20). Later, when he is trying yet again to persuade his siblings to faithfulness, Nephi emphasizes the particular value of Isaiah's words for them, just before he quotes two entire chapters verbatim:

> Hear ye the words of the prophet,
> ye who are a remnant of the house of Israel,
> a branch who have been broken off;
> hear ye the words of the prophet,
> which were written unto all the house of Israel,
> and liken them unto yourselves
> that ye may have hope . . .
> for after this manner hath the prophet written.
> (1 Nephi 19:23–24)

We as Latter-day Saints sometimes forget that more than two-thirds of Nephi's writings are devoted specifically to connecting his family's history with Isaiah's theme of God's plan for the salvation of Israel.[1] It is in Nephi's nonnarrative chapters of doctrinal discourse, scriptural quotation, and original prophecy that we come to know his concerns most intimately. Nephi's primary persona here is as a *reader,* poring over passages included on the brass plates, offering alternative explanations

1. As an illustration: How many depictions of Nephi portray him reading scripture, as opposed to confronting Laban, building a ship, or chastising his brothers? The only one we have been able to identify is the work of Jorge Cocco, an Argentinean LDS artist who, like Arnold Friberg, Minerva Teichert, and Walter Rane, has done a series of paintings illustrating Book of Mormon scenes. Cocco's painting portrays Lehi and his sons reviewing the brass plates. See http://www.jorgecocco.com/big34.jpg, retrieved June 22, 2010.

of their meaning, interweaving his own prophecies with them, and envisioning himself as the author of still future scripture. He professes a love for these writings,[2] and he structures his writings in such a way as to suggest that he is carefully reworking original documents—something we will see in 1 Nephi 22 and 2 Nephi 26–27 in particular.

1 Nephi 22

Nephi's interpretive concerns seem to have been rooted first and foremost in the fact that he had foreseen, in a remarkable, angelically guided vision (reported in 1 Nephi 11–14), the future of his family and the grand sweep of Book of Mormon history. On at least three separate occasions in his record, he connects this revelation to the broader context of God's plan for Israel by tying his own revelation to the written prophecies of others. Not surprisingly, it is always to Isaiah that he first turns for corroboration. He refers to Isaiah's writings as he attempts to explain God's providential plan to Laman and Lemuel (1 Nephi 19:22; see also 15:20), and then he quotes Isaiah 48–49 as evidence (1 Nephi 20–21). When his brothers, like many modern readers, admit that they do not quite understand his point, Nephi responds with a prophecy of his own in 1 Nephi 22 that reiterates the familiar scenario of the house of Israel first being scattered among all nations and then eventually restored to both the lands of their inheritance and the knowledge of Jesus Christ through the instrumentality of latter-day Gentiles.

What makes 1 Nephi 22 striking from a literary perspective is the almost musical way in which Nephi interlaces his own prophecy with phrases from the scriptural chapters he has just quoted. A page from the *Reader's Edition* of the Book of Mormon shows the quotations from Isaiah in italics, highlighting—as it were—the melody line that Nephi is embellishing (see fig. 2).[3] Notice that not only does Nephi provide explicit interpretations for expressions like "lift up mine hand to the

2. In the introduction to the so-called psalm of Nephi, he writes: "my soul delighteth in the scriptures / and my heart pondereth them / and writeth them for the learning and the profit of my children" (2 Nephi 4:15).

3. Grant Hardy, ed., *The Book of Mormon: A Reader's Edition* (Urbana and Chicago: University of Illinois Press, 2003).

58 1 NEPHI 22:6–14

6“Nevertheless, after they shall be ‘*nursed*’[a] by the Gentiles, and the Lord has ‘*lifted up his hand upon the Gentiles and set them up for a standard,*’ and ‘*their children have been carried in their arms, and their daughters have been carried upon their shoulders,*’[b] behold, these things of which are spoken are temporal; for thus are the covenants of the Lord with our fathers; and it meaneth us in the days to come, and also all our brethren who are of the House of Israel. 7And it meaneth that the time cometh that after all the House of Israel have been scattered and confounded, that the Lord God will raise up a ‘*mighty*’[c] nation among the Gentiles, yea, even upon the face of this land; and by them shall our seed be scattered. 8And after our seed is scattered the Lord God will ‘*proceed to do a marvelous work*’[d] among the Gentiles, which shall be of great worth unto our seed; wherefore, it is likened unto their being ‘*nourished by the Gentiles and being carried in their arms and upon their shoulders.*’[e]

9“And it shall also be of worth unto the Gentiles; and not only unto the Gentiles but unto all the House of Israel, unto the making known of the covenants of the Father of Heaven unto Abraham, saying, ‘In thy seed shall all the kindreds of the earth be blessed.’[f] 10And I would, my brethren, that ye should know that all the kindreds of the earth cannot be blessed unless he shall ‘*make bare his arm in the eyes of the nations.*’[g] 11Wherefore, the Lord God will proceed to ‘*make bare his arm in the eyes of all the nations,*’ in bringing about his covenants and his gospel unto those who are of the House of Israel. 12Wherefore, he will bring them again out of captivity, and they shall be gathered together to the lands of their inheritance; and they shall be brought ‘*out of obscurity and out of darkness*’;[h] and they shall ‘*know that the Lord is their Savior and their Redeemer, the Mighty One of Israel.*’[i]

13“And the blood of that great and abominable church, which is the whore of all the earth, shall turn upon their own heads; for they shall war among themselves, and the sword of their own hands shall fall upon their own heads, and ‘*they shall be drunken with their own blood.*’[j] 14And every nation which shall war against thee, O House of Israel, shall be turned one against another, and they shall fall into the pit which they digged to ensnare the people of the Lord. And

[a]6 1 Nephi 21:23 (Isaiah).
[b]6 1 Nephi 21:22 (Isaiah).
[c]7 1 Nephi 21:24–25 (Isaiah).
[d]8 Isaiah 29:14.
[e]8 1 Nephi 21:22 (Isaiah).
[f]9 Genesis 22:18. Cf. Acts 3:25; 1 Nephi 19:17 (Zenos).
[g]10 Isaiah 52:10. Another phrase from this verse is cited at 1 Nephi 19:17.
[h]12 Isaiah 29:18.
[i]12 1 Nephi 21:26 (Isaiah).
[j]13 Ibid.

Figure 2. A passage from 1 Nephi 22 showing Nephi’s interlacing use of quotations from Isaiah in italics. From Grant Hardy, ed., *The Book of Mormon: A Reader’s Edition* (Urbana: University of Illinois Press, 2003).

Gentiles," the "mighty" from whom the Lord will one day deliver captives, and "carried . . . upon their shoulders" (1 Nephi 22:6–8; cf. 21:22, 26), but he also inserts distinct, just-quoted phrases in less obtrusive ways, as when he indicates that latter-day Israel shall "know that the Lord is their Savior and their Redeemer, the Mighty One of Israel" in verse 12, or that wicked latter-day Gentiles shall "be drunken with their own blood" in verse 13 (cf. 1 Nephi 21:26).

Isaiah's prophecies here were originally about the restoration of the Jews to the lands of their inheritance after the Babylonian captivity (something still in the future when Nephi was writing), but Nephi sees these words as also being applicable to the situation of the Lamanites and the Jews in the last days. In order to convey his message, he pulls Isaiah's words from their original context and gives them a new one, much as Mozart spun his own variation from a familiar tune. After we see Isaiah's prophecies in the new setting that Nephi has provided, we understand them differently. The words have not changed, though we now perceive fresh and fuller meanings.

2 Nephi 25–30

But as effective as the variation of a new context can be in expanding an original theme, it is still a pretty simple technique; both of our composers are capable of much more dexterity as the situation warrants. In Mozart's case, consider, for example, the remarkable finale of the first act of the opera *Don Giovanni.* Giovanni here is hosting a feast for everyone who lives in his domain, including the nobility, the bourgeoisie, and the peasants. Mozart represents this moment, amazingly, with the simultaneous performance of three independent dance ensembles—one for each of the social classes (see fig. 3). Again for those who can read music, the score displays his truly ingenious interweaving of three orchestras—each playing in a different time signature. As music critic Robert Harris describes it:

> The minuet we heard before begins again, introducing a section where all the characters comment on what they see and hear. On stage two other orchestras first tune

Figure 3. Mozart's score for *Don Giovanni* incorporates musical themes for three different dance movements.

> up, then play their own dances—a country dance and a waltz—an incredible moment. Here is Mozart at his most complex, playful, and dramatic all at the same time. He has three different dances going, one in the orchestra proper and two on stage, as well as interweaving the thoughts of the six characters as they comment on the action unfolding before them.[4]

Similarly, Isaiah 48–49 is not the only source Nephi draws upon in 1 Nephi 22. In explaining to Laman and Lemuel the role that latter-day Gentiles will play in bringing their (Laman's and Lemuel's) posterity to salvation, Nephi simultaneously incorporates phrases from several additional brass plates texts, including in verse 8, Joseph of Egypt's prophecy about a Gentile work "of great worth," recorded in 2 Nephi 3:7; in verse 9, the Lord's promise to Abraham that one day all nations would participate in his blessing, from Genesis 22:18; in verses 15, 23, and 24, Zenos' prophecies regarding the latter-day gathering of scattered Israel; and in verse 20, the identification of the Holy One of Israel as the new prophet whose coming Moses anticipated in Deuteronomy 18:18–19. Also interwoven are several distinct phrases from Isaiah's prophecy in Isaiah 29 regarding the sealed book, including "proceed to do a marvelous work," "out of obscurity and darkness," "fight against Zion," and "brought low in the dust" (1 Nephi 22:8, 12, 14, 19, 23). Much as Mozart brings together three separate musical genres in a complicated interweaving of voices, Nephi here reworks phrases from multiple sources into a kind of bravura prophetic performance.

In 2 Nephi, following his quotation of five chapters from Jacob's writings and thirteen from Isaiah's, Nephi employs a similar interpretive strategy in his commentary in chapters 25–30. He justifies the inclusion of these lengthy prophecies by appealing to the principle of multiple witnesses:

---

4. Robert Harris, *What to Listen for in Mozart* (New York: Simon & Schuster, 1991), 159.

> For verily [Isaiah] saw my Redeemer, even as I have seen him. And my brother Jacob has also seen him as I have seen him; wherefore, I will send their words forth unto my children to prove unto them that my words are true. Wherefore, "by the words of three," God hath said, "I will establish my word." Nevertheless, God sendeth more witnesses, and he proveth all his words. (2 Nephi 11:2–3)

In keeping with this explanation, Nephi has included, in his interpretive commentary in 2 Nephi 25–30, multiple quotations of, allusions to, and echoes of three distinct primary sources: his own vision in 1 Nephi 11–14; Jacob's interpretations of Isaiah in 2 Nephi 6–10; and Isaiah's prophecies concerning the house of Israel, quoted in 2 Nephi 12–24. Here, too, he integrates at least a dozen other brass plates passages into the new context of his own prophecies. Obvious citations are again indicated with italics and footnotes in the *Readers Edition,* but less explicit allusions can be seen as well. Zenos, Moses, Joseph of Egypt, and other Isaiah passages continue to be numbered among Nephi's other witnesses, but the focus of his interpretation remains on the monumental vision he had previously seen of the future of Israel's Lehite branch (1 Nephi 11–14), which he now presents in terms of the themes of Isaiah 2–14.

This extended quotation from Isaiah originally dealt with Israel's unfaithfulness to her covenants and God's resulting judgments upon her during both the Syro-Ephraimite War of 734 BC and the invasion of Judah by Sennacherib in 701. As Nephi well knew, Isaiah's predictions of Assyria's invasion had been fulfilled a century before, and despite the destruction, a remnant of Judah and a few fleeing Ephraimites had been saved. One of Nephi's purposes, then, in this lengthy excerpt is to affirm the validity of prophecy itself, namely, that everything the Lord has revealed will indeed come to pass.

In Nephi's reading, however, Isaiah's prophecies are not just predicting specific events regarding the fall of Samaria. Now that Judah has likewise become corrupt, Nephi has seen that God will again mete out righteous judgment, this time via Babylon, and will once again preserve a remnant—including his own family. In Isaiah's prophecies,

Nephi recognizes a typological pattern for God's dealings with the house of Israel throughout the duration of human history, a pattern of judgment and salvation to be repeated over and over:

> I write unto . . . all those that shall receive hereafter these things . . . that they may know the judgments of God, that they come upon all nations, according to the word which he hath spoken. . . . And as one generation hath been destroyed among the Jews because of iniquity, even so have they been destroyed from generation to generation according to their iniquities, and never hath any of them been destroyed save it were foretold them by the prophets of the Lord. (2 Nephi 25:3, 9)

In 2 Nephi 25–30, Nephi interprets "plainly" this pattern of judgment at the heart of Israel's story, likening the oppression of the Egyptians to the subsequent destructions wrought against Israel in the Old World by the Assyrians, the Babylonians, and eventually the Romans; and against an Israelite remnant in the New World first by God himself at the time of the "great and terrible storm" of Jesus's crucifixion, then by the Lamanites about AD 400, and finally by the Gentile nations in the latter days. But central to Nephi's argument is that, at every iteration, Isaiah's pattern also includes the salvation of a remnant. And he prophesies here that in the case of the Lehites, this remnant will include a text as well as a people. Someday, the very record that Nephi is composing—with its emphatic testimony of Jesus Christ—will be instrumental in bringing both unity and salvation to latter-day Israel.

We can discern Nephi's general methodology for interpreting scripture from these two great prophetic discourses (that is, from 1 Nephi 22 and 2 Nephi 25–30). In each, he follows the direct quotation of an extended passage from Isaiah with an interpretive discussion that incorporates both themes and key phrases but does not provide a comprehensive or detailed commentary on Isaiah's words. Instead, he works the phrases into a fresh prophecy that recontextualizes and expands the meaning of the Isaianic original with particular reference to the future of his own people. Nephi uses the words of Isaiah as a medium through which to communicate his own prophetic understanding of the future, and also as a way to demonstrate that he is in harmony with what the Lord's servants have said before.

2 Nephi 26–27

At this point, it is perhaps necessary to complicate the comparison between Nephi and Mozart because Nephi is at times more a performer than a composer of scripture. It is always a pleasure to hear a fine musician play one of Mozart's piano concertos. Of course, the notes themselves are virtually identical from performance to performance, but each soloist is able to put an individual stamp on the work through phrasing, timing, and attack. In fact, there is a sense in which the same piece can convey different meaning over time. It is odd to think that Mozart was once considered difficult music—avant-garde and hard to listen to—but those first audiences had never heard Beethoven, let alone Bartok or Schoenberg. Different contexts can dramatically shift the way that music is understood, just as putting Isaiah into Nephi's hands can greatly expand our appreciation of his foresight.

The most significant example of Nephi's reworking of biblical prophecy comes in such a moment of scriptural performance (rather than composition), at a point in 2 Nephi 25–30 where he follows a slightly different rhetorical approach than what we saw in 1 Nephi 22. Instead of first quoting Isaiah and then borrowing themes and occasional phrases for a fresh prophetic elaboration, here Nephi incorporates the entirety of Isaiah 29:3–24 into his own predictions of forthcoming judgment and salvation. In 2 Nephi 26–27 Nephi is performing Isaiah's score, weaving his own interpretation into his predecessor's framework rather than other way around. And only here is his appropriation of Isaiah's writings complete, suggesting perhaps that unlike other Isaianic prophecies that anticipate multiple fulfillments, Nephi understood this prediction to be aimed at a singular, particular fulfillment in the future, one whose previously obscure interpretation is clarified by Nephi's revelation and plainness in prophesying.

In these chapters, Nephi's commentary on Isaiah is interlinear—he writes, as it were, between the borrowed lines. This can be seen by comparing the text of 2 Nephi 26:14–19, again taken from the *Reader's Edition* with its italicization of the words of Isaiah, with Isaiah 29:3–5 (as found in the King James Version):

> I will camp against thee round about, and will lay siege against thee with a mount, and I will raise forts against thee. And thou shalt be brought down, and shalt speak out of the ground, and thy speech shall be low out of the dust, and thy voice shall be, as of one that hath a familiar spirit, out of the ground, and thy speech shall whisper out of the dust. Moreover the multitude of thy strangers

The Lehites in the Last Days (Midrash on Isaiah 29:3–5)[b]

14But behold, I prophesy unto you concerning the last days; concerning the days when the Lord God shall bring these things forth unto the children of men.
15After my seed and the seed of my brethren shall have dwindled in unbelief, and shall have been smitten by the Gentiles; yea, after the Lord God shall have *camped against them round about,* and shall have *laid seige against them with a mount,* and *raised forts against them;* and after they *shall have been brought down* low in the dust, even that they are not, yet the words of the righteous shall be written, and the prayers of the faithful shall be heard, and all those who have dwindled in unbelief shall not be forgotten. 16For those who shall be destroyed
shall speak unto them out of the ground, and their speech shall be low out of the dust, and their voice shall be as one that hath a familiar spirit; for the Lord God will give unto him power, that he may whisper concerning them, even as it were *out of the ground;* and their *speech shall whisper out of the dust.*
17For thus saith the Lord God, "They shall write the things which shall be done among them, and they shall be written and sealed up in a book, and those who have dwindled in unbelief shall not have them, for they seek to destroy the things of God." 18Wherefore, as those who have been destroyed have been destroyed speedily; and *the multitude of their terrible ones shall be as chaff that pas-*

[a]10 Isaiah 52:3.
[b]14 Note that the italicized phrases in verses 14–19 reproduce Isaiah 29:3–5. Most of Isaiah 29, in order, is interspersed in 2 Nephi 26:14–27:35.

Figure 4. This passage from 2 Nephi 26 shows Nephi's interlinear commentary on Isaiah 29. From Hardy, *Reader's Edition*.

Table 1. Distribution of Isaiah 29 in 2 Nephi 26–27

2 Nephi	Isaiah		# of verses added
26:14–19	29:3–5	slightly expanded quotation	3
26:20–33		additional comments by Nephi	14
27:1–5	29:6–10	slightly expanded quotation	0
27:6–23	29:11–12	greatly expanded quotation	16
27:24–35	29:13–24	nearly exact quotation	0

> shall be like small dust, and the multitude of the terrible ones shall be as chaff that passeth away: yea, it shall be at an instant suddenly.

Notice that nearly all the key phrases from Isaiah 29 have been integrated here, in the order in which they originally appeared. The correspondence is clearly deliberate on Nephi's part.[5]

The rest of Isaiah 29:6–12 keeps coming piece by piece, through the rest of this chapter and the next, with an increasing amount of commentary. But then suddenly, at 2 Nephi 27:24, Nephi is back on script, this time quoting Isaiah (now from 29:13–24) so closely that we can arrange the passage into the poetic lines appropriate to Isaiah's original style. Over the course of fifty-five verses, Nephi quotes twenty-two verses from Isaiah 29 while interspersing an additional thirty-three verses of his own interpretation, so that his integration looks something like that shown in table 1.

In many ways, the second and fourth sections here are the most interesting. These are where Nephi departs most drastically from his

5. It should be noted that Book of Mormon commentators have been quick to assume that Nephi is, in 2 Nephi 26–27, restoring the original text of Isaiah 29—and justification is often made with reference to the Joseph Smith Translation of Isaiah 29. Obviously, we are here approaching the text in another way, presuming that the King James Version of Isaiah 29 represents more or less the text Nephi had before him, and that 2 Nephi 26–27 therefore represents Nephi's creative adaptation of and variation on the Isaianic text, rather than his reproduction of an original that has otherwise been lost.

underlying source material, adding the most by way of explanation to the verses he quotes. These largely "off-script" comments, at 2 Nephi 26:20–33 and at 27:6–23, offer the clearest picture of how Nephi reads Isaiah 29 and then shapes his readers' perceptions of the text. We will consider each of them in turn.

Perhaps the most dramatic moment in a Mozart piano concerto comes right before the end of the first movement, in a section called the *cadenza*. Here, by tradition, the orchestra drops out and the pianist is given space to improvise, to go off-script as it were. In the score, it does not look like much—just one chord in a single measure, followed by fermatas in the orchestral parts. Fermatas, as you recall, are variable rests, and sometimes the orchestra will rest for a full minute, or three minutes, or even five minutes as the soloist weaves together new musical ideas with familiar themes in what is often the most virtuosic part of the entire concerto. When the orchestra finally rejoins the performer for a few recognizable motifs in the coda, the audience can often hear them in a fresh way. Something has changed, not in the melody itself, but in our perception of it. We might think of these two sections in 2 Nephi 26–27 as Nephi's cadenzas: his performance of Isaiah continues, but here Nephi, as soloist, has the opportunity to display his own virtuosic interpretation.

2 Nephi 26:20–33

How, then, does Nephi shape his readers' perceptions of Isaiah in his first improvised section, at 2 Nephi 26:20–33? At first glance, it seems completely intelligible to cut directly from 2 Nephi 26:19 to 27:1, where his direct adaptation of Isaiah 29 resumes—that is, to entirely skip Nephi's independent commentary. But on closer inspection, some problems emerge when the intervening verses are omitted. The first thing to note is that in Nephi's presentation, as opposed to Isaiah's, the context has shifted dramatically from 26:19, where the focus is on the fratricidal destruction of the Nephites in AD 400, to 27:1, where the focus is instead on the pending destruction of the Gentile nations in the last days. One purpose, obviously, of Nephi's "off-script" material is to ease this transition. But he also intervenes to forestall misunderstandings of particular passages in the Isaiah text that follows. For example, the impression we receive from both 2 Nephi 26:15 and 27:2 is that the Lord of Hosts is a god of judgment, vengeance, and punishment. Yet in his off-script commentary between these two passages, Nephi makes clear that God is actually best characterized by his compassion: "he doeth not anything save it be for the benefit of the world" (26:24), and he invites all humankind to come and "partake of his goodness" (26:33). Nephi does not want his readers to attach blame to the wrong party when they resume their reading of Isaiah 29 in chapter 27.

In like manner, Nephi's description in his off-script commentary of self-satisfied, latter-day Gentiles also shapes our subsequent perceptions. When we get to the Lord's admonition against the "wise and the learned" in the quotation of Isaiah 29:13–14 (in 2 Nephi 27:24–25), the antecedent is the learned book-reader adapted from Isaiah 29:12. Without the prior criticism of Gentiles who "preach unto themselves their own wisdom and their own learning" (2 Nephi 26:20), we might be tempted to see the learned man in question—whom we have come to recognize as Charles Anthon—as the sole villain of the prophecy. But his is simply a walk-on role; Nephi makes us aware in advance that he is representative of a much more pervasive problem.

Like any good improvising soloist, Nephi also provides in this cadenza an indication of where the performance is headed. His comment at 2 Nephi 26:17 that the Nephites would write and seal up a book before being destroyed anticipates the extended discussion of that book in chapter 27. Similarly, Nephi's comments on the role of Gentile churches and the influence of the devil in the last days (26:20–22) anticipate chapter 28. And his equivalence of Jew and Gentile in the final verse of his cadenza foreshadows the end of his larger discourse that culminates in a prophecy about the uniting of the two groups in the Messianic age (chapters 29–30).

Between his two cadenzas, when he returns directly to Isaiah's words in the first verses of 2 Nephi 27, Nephi begins again to play Isaiah like a musical score, with his own accents and articulation. In Nephi's telling it is not Zion, but rather the nations of the Gentiles who fight against her that will be visited by the Lord with natural disasters (2 Nephi 27:2; cf. Isaiah 29:6). He also clarifies that it is the Gentiles' iniquities and not the Lord's indifference that has resulted in their gross lack of understanding (2 Nephi 27:5; cf. Isaiah 29:10). Moreover, Nephi continues to prepare his readers to interpret ambiguities in these verses in a particular way. Isaiah, for example, writes of people who are "drunken but not with wine" (2 Nephi 27:4 // Isaiah 29:9). Readers of Nephi's version have no need to speculate about the meaning of this odd expression—are they confused? disoriented? insensible?—since he has previously described the latter-day Gentiles as "drunken *with iniquity*" (2 Nephi 27:1) and adds two more references to "iniquity" (in verses 4 and 5) between Isaiah's lines. If the interpretation of "drunken" as "drunken with iniquity" seems obvious to readers of 2 Nephi 27, it is because Nephi has made it so. What is more, we do not need to puzzle over the nature of this spiritual stupor—asking whether it is the result of confusion or religious fundamentalism or political accommodation. Nephi has already listed the iniquities in question at 2 Nephi 26:32.

2 Nephi 27:6–23

As we move on to Nephi's second largely improvised section, it is clear that something extraordinary is happening in his citation of Isaiah 29:11–12. Note first the very low density of italicized phrases (see figs. 5 and 6). This is where Nephi is expanding key phrases from the two following verses of Isaiah's by sixteen more:

> And the vision of all is become unto you as the words of a book that is sealed, which men deliver to one that is learned, saying, Read this, I pray thee: and he saith, I cannot; for it is sealed: And the book is delivered to him that is not learned, saying, Read this, I pray thee: and he saith, I am not learned.

From this brief passage, Nephi launches into a breathtaking digression that will reshape the way we see the entire chapter.

Interestingly, in modern translations of the Bible that set Isaiah into poetic lines, verses 11–12 are distinct because they are in prose, and they stick out as such; indeed, many scholars have suggested that

2 NEPHI 27:6–15 125

A Sealed Book (Midrash on Isaiah 29:11–12)[a]

[6]And it shall come to pass that the Lord God shall bring forth unto you *the words of a book,* and they shall be the words of them which have slumbered. [7]And behold, the book *shall be sealed;* and in the book shall be a revelation from God, from the beginning of the world to the ending thereof.[b] [8]Wherefore, because of the things which are sealed up, the things which are sealed shall not be delivered in the day of the wickedness and abominations of the people. Wherefore the book shall be kept from them.

[9]But the book shall be delivered unto a man, and he shall deliver the words of the book, which are the words of those who have slumbered in the dust, and he shall *deliver* these words unto another; [10]but the words which are sealed he shall not deliver, neither shall he deliver the book. For the book shall be sealed by the power of God, and the revelation which was sealed shall be kept in the book until the own due time of the Lord, that they may come forth; for behold, they reveal all things from the foundation of the world unto the end thereof. [11]And the day cometh that the words of the book which were sealed shall be read upon the house tops; and they shall be read by the power of Christ; and all things shall be revealed unto the children of men which ever have been among the children of men, and which ever will be even unto the end of the earth.

[12]Wherefore, at that day when the book shall be delivered unto the man of whom I have spoken, the book shall be hid from the eyes of the world, that the eyes of none shall behold it, save it be that three witnesses shall behold it by the power of God, besides him to whom the book shall be delivered; and they shall testify to the truth of the book and the things therein.[c] [13]And there is none other which shall view it, save it be a few according to the will of God, to bear testimony of his word unto the children of men;[d] for the Lord God hath said that the words of the faithful should speak as if it were from the dead. [14]Wherefore, the Lord God will proceed to bring forth the words of the book; and in the mouth of as many witnesses as seemeth him good will he establish his word; and wo be unto him that rejecteth the word of God!

[15]But behold, it shall come to pass that the Lord God shall say unto him to whom he shall deliver the book, "Take these words which are not sealed and deliver them to another, that he may show them *unto the learned, saying: 'Read*

[a]6 The prophecies in this section were fulfilled when Martin Harris took some characters copied from the Gold Plates to Professor Charles Anthon in New York City in 1828. See "Joseph Smith—History" 1:62–65; and appendix 2.

[b]7 This apparently refers to the sealed portion of the Gold Plates. See Ether 3:25–28, 4:5–6.

[c]12 See the "The Testimony of the Three Witnesses" in appendix 1.

[d]13 See "The Testimony of the Eight Witnesses" in appendix 1.

Figure 5. This passage from 2 Nephi 27 is an expansive prophetic interpolation of Isaiah 29:11–12. From Hardy, *Reader's Edition*.

they are later glosses or additions for precisely this reason. Whatever form they may have taken on the brass plates, it is as if Nephi sees those verses and thinks, "Cadenza!" And he takes that moment to insert a prophetic interpolation concerning this sealed book and those who will someday attempt to read it. He begins by identifying Isaiah's "vision of all" with his own prophecy of the revelation of "all things" that have been "written and sealed up to come forth . . . in the own due time of the Lord" (2 Nephi 27:7, 10; cf. 1 Nephi 14:21–22, 26). He then writes of the motivations of the learned and unlearned readers, of the consequences of their actions, and the destiny of the marvelous book.

As before, Nephi seems to be interpreting in advance. At the end of the cadenza, he foretells two statements that the Lord will one day make to Joseph Smith, identified here (by description) as the unlearned man of Isaiah 29:12. The first of these statements, appearing in 2 Nephi 27:20–23 (fig. 6 #1), is introduced simply, "Then shall the Lord God say unto him . . ." with what follows appearing to be a fresh revelation to Nephi (this passage does not have any phrases taken from Isaiah). The second statement, appearing in verses 24–26 (fig. 6 #2), is quoted directly from Isaiah 29:13–15, where it appears as the Lord's general pronouncement on Israel's recalcitrance, though Nephi has applied it to latter-day Gentiles and directed it to Joseph Smith, as is made clear in his inserted introduction: "And again it shall come to pass that the Lord shall say unto him that shall read the words that shall be delivered him."

Anticipatorily, Nephi has already worked significant phrases from both of these statements into the earlier part of his "off-script" discussion, apparently to forestall any misapprehension that might have arisen from reading the statements cold. All of the underlined terms in figure 7 were predefined by Nephi. For example, in 2 Nephi 27:6–14, Nephi had explained several otherwise ambiguous terms from these directives, including the words that are to be read, the sealed things that are not to be touched, the witnesses that have been promised, the subsequent resealing of the book, and the specific meaning of "all things" that are to be revealed at some future time. (Additional overlapping words and phrases include "mine own due time" and the equation of the Lord "proceed[ing] to bring forth the words of the book," which

126 2 NEPHI 27:16–27

this, I pray thee.' And the learned *shall say,* 'Bring hither the book, and I will read
them.' [16]And now, because of the glory of the world and to get gain will they
say this, and not for the glory of God. [17]And the man shall say, '*I cannot* bring
the book, *for it is sealed.*' [18]Then shall the learned say, 'I cannot read it.'"

[19]Wherefore it shall come to pass, that the Lord God will *deliver again the
book* and the words thereof *to him that is not learned; and* the man that is not
learned *shall say, "I am not learned."* [20]Then shall the Lord God say unto him,
"The learned shall not read them, for they have rejected them, and I am able to
do mine own work; wherefore thou shalt read the words which I shall give unto
thee. [21]Touch not the things which are sealed, for I will bring them forth in mine
own due time; for I will show unto the children of men that I am able to do mine
own work. [22]Wherefore, when thou hast read the words which I have command-
ed thee, and obtained the witnesses which I have promised unto thee, then shalt
#1 thou seal up the book again, and hide it up unto me, that I may preserve the
words which thou hast not read, until I shall see fit in mine own wisdom to reveal
all things unto the children of men. [23]For behold, I am God; and I am a God of
miracles; and I will show unto the world that I am the same yesterday, today,
and forever; and I work not among the children of men save it be according to
their faith."

The Lord Knows and Judges (Isaiah 29:13–24)[a]

[24]And again it shall come to pass that the Lord shall say unto him that shall
read the words that shall be delivered him:

[25]"Forasmuch as this people draw near unto me with their mouth,
and with their lips do honor me,
but have removed their hearts far from me,
#2 and their fear towards me is taught by the precepts of men—
[26]Therefore, I will proceed to do a marvelous work among this people,
yea, a marvelous work and a wonder,
for the wisdom of their wise and learned shall perish,
and the understanding of their prudent shall be hid."

[27]And wo unto them that seek deep to hide their counsel from the Lord!
And their works are in the dark;
and they say, "Who seeth us, and who knoweth us?"
And they also say, "Surely, your turning of things upside down
shall be esteemed as the potter's clay."

[a]24 This section of Isaiah 29 is quoted directly, so it is not italicized.

Figure 6. Underlined text signals passages anticipating what the Lord would say to Joseph Smith, the first Nephi's own prophecy, the second Isaiah's. From Hardy, *Reader's Edition*.

126 2 NEPHI 27:16–27

this, I pray thee.' And the learned *shall say,* 'Bring hither the book, and I will read
them.' [16]And now, because of the glory of the world and to get gain will they
say this, and not for the glory of God. [17]And the man shall say, *'I cannot* bring
the book, *for it is sealed.'* [18]Then shall the learned say, 'I cannot read it.'"

[19]Wherefore it shall come to pass, that the Lord God will *deliver again the
book* and the words thereof *to him that is not learned; and* the man that is not
learned *shall say, "I am not learned."* [20]Then shall the Lord God say unto him,
"The learned shall not read them, for they have rejected them, and I am able to
do mine own work; wherefore thou shalt read the words which I shall give unto
thee. [21]Touch not the things which are sealed, for I will bring them forth in mine
own due time; for I will show unto the children of men that I am able to do mine
own work. [22]Wherefore, when thou hast read the words which I have command-
#1 ed thee, and obtained the witnesses which I have promised unto thee, then shalt
thou seal up the book again, and hide it up unto me, that I may preserve the
words which thou hast not read, until I shall see fit in mine own wisdom to reveal
all things unto the children of men. [23]For behold, I am God; and I am a God of
miracles; and I will show unto the world that I am the same yesterday, today,
and forever; and I work not among the children of men save it be according to
their faith."

The Lord Knows and Judges (Isaiah 29:13–24)[a]

[24]And again it shall come to pass that the Lord shall say unto him that shall
read the words that shall be delivered him:

[25]"Forasmuch as this people draw near unto me with their mouth,
and with their lips do honor me,
but have removed their hearts far from me,
#2 and their fear towards me is taught by the precepts of men—
[26]Therefore, I will proceed to do a marvelous work among this people,
yea, a marvelous work and a wonder,
for the wisdom of their wise and learned shall perish,
and the understanding of their prudent shall be hid."

[27]And wo unto them that seek deep to hide their counsel from the Lord!
And their works are in the dark;
and they say, "Who seeth us, and who knoweth us?"
And they also say, "Surely, your turning of things upside down
shall be esteemed as the potter's clay."

[a]24 This section of Isaiah 29 is quoted directly, so it is not italicized.

Figure 7. It is significant that, earlier in the chapter, Nephi had methodically predefined these underlined phrases from 2 Nephi 27:20–26.

appears in verse 14, with his "proceed[ing] to do a marvelous work and a wonder" later in verse 26.)

2 Nephi 27:24–35

If our task here is to read Nephi reading Isaiah, as if Nephi were onstage performing an Isaiah concerto, what are we to make of the coda—that is, of the part where, after going off-score for some prophetic improvisation, Nephi suddenly returns to the text of Isaiah 29, basically as written? At first glance, the last section of 2 Nephi 27, which quotes Isaiah 29:13–24 nearly verbatim, seems like an interruption. The bulk of the passage addresses reversals: the cedars of Lebanon will become a field; the blind will see; the poor will rejoice; the terrible one will be brought to naught; Jacob (the house of Israel), who was once ashamed, will praise God when he sees his posterity and God's work among them; and, finally, those who erred in spirit will come to understanding. What are we to make of this series? Have we abandoned Nephi's concerns in a return to the political controversies of Isaiah's day, or are these reversals eschatological in nature, pointing to some vague but glorious future?

Whatever our impressions, the entire passage seems to represent a significant departure from the two primary themes we followed in 2 Nephi 26–27—those of the latter-day Gentiles and the sealed book. The fact that these two themes are again picked up at the beginning of chapter 28, immediately following the quotation, suggests either that the whole of 2 Nephi 27:24–35 is extraneous or that there is a closer thematic connection between the quotation and its context in Nephi's record than meets the eye. Given both the presumed difficulty of engraving upon the plates and Nephi's self-consciously intentional writing in this discourse (cf. 2 Nephi 25:1–7), the real question posed to readers here is why he includes Isaiah 29:13–24 at all.

It is possible that Nephi is, in fact, using Isaiah's words to continue his discussion of the relationship between the latter-day Gentiles and the sealed book—at least part of which will become the future Book of Mormon. Verse 27, which speaks of some confusion in distinguishing the producer from the product is the first key to such an interpretation: "For shall the work say of him that made it, 'He made me not'? Or shall the thing framed say of him that framed it, 'He hath no understanding'?" To most outsiders, the Book of Mormon—with its theological anachronisms, awkward diction, and lengthy quotations from the King James Bible—emphatically signals, *I was not made by an ancient prophet named Mormon.* The evidence of forgery, for them, is so obvious that it hardly merits discussion, and they assume that the text itself stands as sufficient evidence that Joseph Smith had no understanding. But if Nephi intended verse 27 as a reference to the Book of Mormon, then this dismissive attribution in itself represents a "turning of things upside down" (2 Nephi 27:27), and the rest of the passage falls into place.

Building on this interpretation, we can read Nephi's gloss in the same verse ("'But behold, I will show unto them,' saith the Lord of Hosts, 'that I know all their works'") as suggesting further that God knows exactly what these faithless latter-day Gentiles are up to. He knows all about their "works in the dark," which they will try to cloak with religion. This "I will show" insert (repeated in verse 28 as "I will show unto the children of men . . .") may also be echoing an earlier statement from the Lord at 27:21 ("I will show unto the children of men that I am able to do mine own work"), thereby identifying who the "potter" or "framer" of the sealed book truly is: the God of Israel.

Another way to discern Nephi's intention in including this passage is to identify its verbal connections with his interpretive comments both preceding and following the quotation. For example, the "wo" statement that begins verse 27 will be extended into a list of woes in the next chapter (28:15–29). Those who "seek deep to hide their counsel from the Lord" are later identified by Nephi as latter-day Gentiles (28:9), and their "works . . . in the dark" echo the "works of darkness" mentioned back in 26:22, which are again explicitly identified with latter-day Gentiles in 28:9. The status of the poor and the meek, mentioned in 27:30, is also described in 26:20 and 28:11–14, and the promise that "they that erred in spirit shall come to understanding" (27:35) echoes Nephi's earlier assertion that because of the plainness of his own prophecies "no man can err" (25:7). Likewise, the follow-up statement in verse 35 that "they that murmured shall learn doctrine" contrasts with the false doctrines and "precepts of men" described in both chapters 26 and 28.

There is, at the very least, good reason to suggest that Nephi's inclusion of Isaiah 29:13–24 is intentional. But two phrases in particular from Isaiah's list of reversals stand out for their potential thematic significance. The first, in 2 Nephi 27:29, indicates that "the deaf [shall] hear the words of the book," a reference that seems to refer back to the sealed book of 27:6-23, to the same book that Nephi describes after he completes his quotation as being "of great worth unto the children of men, and especially unto our seed" (2 Nephi 28:2). Nephi's framing here suggests that the book itself will be the cause of the reversals that follow: the (spiritually) blind will see, the oppressed will find joy, and scoffers and critics who seize upon minutiae will come to nothing. The descendants of Jacob will recover their dignity and return to the correct worship of God, and, because of the Book of Mormon itself, many who have gone astray will find the truth.

But it is Nephi's interpretation of a second phrase from the list of reversals that most clearly demonstrates his reading of Isaiah. Among those whose fortunes will change, Isaiah tells us, are they that "turn aside the just for a thing of naught" (2 Nephi 27:32). Nephi transfers this phrase directly into one of his "wo comments" in the following chapter, in a passage that echoes both Isaiah 29 and his prior description of the book to be revealed in latter days: "Wo unto them that 'turn aside the just for a thing of naught,' and revile against that which is good, and say, 'That is of no worth!'" (2 Nephi 28:16).[6] When he writes of those who "revile against that which is good," he is speaking of the wise, learned, and rich Gentiles who will reject the Book of Mormon, and when he equates that action with "turning aside the just for a thing of naught," it appears that he is, in fact, reading "the just" in 27:32 as a kind of code word for the people associated with that book—its authors, translator, believers, or perhaps even for the book itself.

6. Throughout Nephi's writings, when he speaks of something having "worth" or "great worth," it is usually a reference to Joseph's prophecy of the Book of Mormon at 2 Nephi 3:7.

Conclusions

We would like to conclude by responding to two related questions. First, how does Nephi read Isaiah? And second, how does he thereby shape his readers' perceptions of the prophet's words?

As far as reading goes, Nephi's signature strategy is to use his own vision of God's providential plan for the Lehites (from 1 Nephi 11–14) as a template for understanding the destiny of the entire house of Israel. Into this framework, Nephi fits particular passages from Isaiah and other brass plates prophets, and, in the subsequent extrapolation from the part to the whole, he articulates a comprehensive sequence of anticipated events—not only for his own people, but for Israel and the Gentile nations as well. In doing so, Nephi affirms his expectation of a temporal, that is, of an "according-to-the flesh" (1 Nephi 22:2, 18, 27), fulfillment of prophecy.

With his reading of Israel's future in place, Nephi shapes his readers' perceptions of Isaiah in the following ways:

1. He quotes extended blocks of text (such as Isaiah 48–49 or Isaiah 2–14) and then incorporates their general themes and particular passages into his own commentary in an articulation of his comprehensive prophetic scheme and as evidence of the validity of his extrapolation. He and Isaiah, Nephi is telling us, saw the same truth.
2. Nephi provides corroborating evidence for his interpretations by integrating the prophecies of multiple witnesses into his account. He alludes to additional writings from Isaiah, his brother Jacob, and several brass plates' prophets. He acknowledges this strategy explicitly in 2 Nephi 11.[7]
3. Nephi also explicitly acknowledges his intention to interpret "plainly," and he does so by defining ambiguities in terms of specific historical expectations, as when he explains Isaiah's "even the captives of the mighty shall be taken away" (Isaiah 49:25, quoted at 1 Nephi 21:25) in

7. As noted before, the *Reader's Edition* makes many of these borrowings clear.

terms of the "mighty" Gentile nation that will in latter days possess the Lehite land of promise; or, more extensively, when he identifies "the book" of Isaiah 29 as the record that his own people will produce. As we saw in 2 Nephi 26–27, he sometimes defines such terms in advance of their quotation in order to forestall reader misperceptions.

4. Nephi also on occasion shifts the objects or addressees of Isaiah's prophecies. Sometimes this is the result of his recontextualization of Isaiah's texts concerning (what for Nephi was) Israel's past within his own interests regarding the Lehite future. On other occasions it is blatant reappropriation, as when he asserts that the Lord of Hosts will destroy not Zion, but those that fight against her in 2 Nephi 27:2 (cf. Isaiah 29:6).
5. On at least one occasion, Nephi shapes his readers' perceptions of a passage from Isaiah by interpretive framing. We came to recognize the passage about radical reversals from Isaiah 29 as describing the changes that would result from the coming forth of the Book of Mormon primarily from Nephi's positioning of this quotation between commentary on the twin themes of the latter-day Gentiles and the sealed book. Nephi's subsequent exegesis suggests that he intended this interpretation.
6. Finally, Nephi recognizes and explains a typological pattern of multiple fulfillment for some of Isaiah's prophecies, most notably those relating to the Lord's repeated judgment of unrepentant Israel followed by the preservation of a righteous remnant. Other prophecies, particularly those relating to the sealed book of Isaiah 29, are portrayed as having a singular, unique fulfillment, and Nephi shapes his readers' perceptions of this in both his direct commentary and his midrashic mode of interlinear quotation.

In the end, we will only understand Isaiah in the Book of Mormon—and what it might contribute to Isaiah in the Hebrew Bible—when we read Nephi's nonnarrative writings as closely as a musician might read a score. In the film *Amadeus,* Antonio Salieri hears a Mozart serenade and exclaims, "It seemed to me that I had heard the voice of God."[8] The playwright Peter Shaffer, of course, uses this comparison of a Mozart piece to the word of God for his own artistic purposes, but there may be a sense in which an inversion of Salieri's exclamation might be instructive: the word of God can sometimes seem quite a bit like a Mozart masterpiece.

8. Peter Shaffer, *Amadeus* (New York: Harper & Row, 1981), 19.

Slumbering Voices: Death and Textuality in 2 Nephi

Jenny Webb

The relationship between Nephi and Isaiah on any level—historical, doctrinal, theological, etc.—is complex. And the relationship between Isaiah 29 and 2 Nephi 26–27 is extraordinarily so. Our goals at the beginning of the collective undertaking of this project appeared somewhat reasonable, perhaps even modest. As formulated in the seminar's discussion questions, we sought to explore the following:

1. How does Nephi adapt Isaiah's text, and what do his methods tell us about what it means to read a scriptural text?
2. What does 2 Nephi 26–27 tell us about the nature of prophecy and scriptural application?
3. How do these chapters provide a clearer understanding of what Nephi is trying to accomplish in his small plates?
4. What does 2 Nephi 26–27 teach us about the nature, role, and place of the Book of Mormon?

In short, part of what we hoped to gain from this experience is an increasingly nuanced and carefully articulated understanding concerning the contours of the *textual* relationship between Nephi and Isaiah. I wish to respond to the first question above by focusing on the thematic development of death throughout chapters 26 and 27 and then considering how Nephi's use of death imagery provides a textual topos for the reading of the Book of Mormon, and indeed, scripture generally.

To begin, I will first provide a brief textual backdrop in order to orient us as we navigate our way through these potentially perilous waters. Within current Mormon scholarship and criticism, the link between Isaiah 29 and 2 Nephi 26–27 is undisputed. Much of this scholarship, however, tends to focus on the doctrinal and theological ties between the texts, explaining the textual relationship as "words . . . spoken to Isaiah centuries before . . . and recorded by Nephi in 2 Nephi."[1] The process identified by Nephi as "likening" the scriptures (see, for example, 1 Nephi 19:23–24; 2 Nephi 11:2, 8) is thus commonly depicted as a re-presenting of the words of a past prophet, in this case, Isaiah. While this process accurately describes the manner in which Nephi inserts Isaiah 2–14 into 2 Nephi 12–24 more or less without (major) alteration, it fails to adequately explain the textual relationship between Isaiah 29 and 2 Nephi 26–27, wherein Nephi appropriates phrases and fragments of the Isaiah text, interweaving them with his own personal prophetic work without identifying their Isaianic source. As can be seen in Appendix 1, Nephi's use of Isaiah's words is substantial, but not necessarily sustained. Isaiah's words are clearly central to Nephi's discussion, but it does not appear that Nephi intends the reader to consciously jump back and forth within his or her reading, here attributing the text to Nephi and there to Isaiah. Indeed, the orthographic texture here instead demands a sort of textual seamlessness between Nephi and Isaiah, a partial erasure of Isaiah's past prophetic identity and authority over the words.

Robert Cloward makes a critical observation concerning the textual relationship at hand that provides us with a way to move toward a thematic or literary discussion of the text. Cloward identifies the relationship between Isaiah 29 and 2 Nephi as extending beyond the more obvious linguistic parallels in chapters 26–27 and, instead, also including Nephi's summary concerning the fate of the Jews in 2 Nephi 25:

---

1. S. Michael Wilcox, "Nephi's Message to the 'Gentiles,'" in *The Book of Mormon: Second Nephi, the Doctrinal Structure*, ed. Monte S. Nyman and Charles D. Tate Jr. (Provo, UT: Religious Studies Center, Brigham Young University, 1989), 277.

> Isaiah 29 is not found in the Book of Mormon where readers usually look, that is, in 2 Nephi 27. The intent and meaning of Isaiah 29 are found in 2 Nephi 25:9–20. This first section of Nephi's "own prophecy" deals with Jerusalem and the Jews, just as Isaiah 29 does. Usually when looking for Isaiah in the Book of Mormon, readers look for Isaiah's actual words. Many words of Isaiah 29 do appear in the second section of Nephi's "own prophecy," *but Nephi has given the words new meaning.* He is no longer speaking of Jerusalem.[2]

The structural insight here is quite useful: Nephi's prophetic interaction with Isaiah 29 occurs on multiple levels—the historical, the doctrinal, the thematic, as well as the linguistic—but it is imperative to recognize that not all such interactions need to occupy the same textual space. Indeed, extending Cloward's discussion a bit further, we might say that Nephi's interaction with Isaiah 29 as a text is experientially fragmented throughout chapters 25–27, with chapter 25 containing the rearticulation or explanation of Isaiah's message in chapter 29, albeit without direct recourse to Isaiah's language, and the following chapters containing Nephi's prophetic experimentation upon the, as it were, now-liberated word, wherein Isaiah's language is appropriated into Nephi's own historical context and doctrinal teachings. It is this movement that I am interested in exploring further: how does one prophet accept the doctrinal content of another prophet's words while simultaneously rejecting, to a degree, the prior prophet's sense of ownership over his own words in an act of appropriation that clears the ground for a new prophetic discourse?[3]

---

2. Robert A. Cloward, "Isaiah 29 and the Book of Mormon," in *Isaiah in the Book of Mormon*, ed. Donald W. Parry and John W. Welch (Provo, UT: FARMS, 1998), 204, emphasis added.

3. Note that I am not arguing that Nephi necessarily understood Isaiah's words in terms of authorial ownership. While we know that Nephi certainly identified Isaiah as author (e.g., "my soul delighteth in the words of Isaiah" [2 Nephi 25:5]), authorship does not equate ownership. The association between authorship and ownership is an admittedly modern development. However, given our own modernity as readers, given

With this textual background and the resulting questions now in mind, let us return to the text of 2 Nephi 26–27 itself. Chapter 26 begins with a subtle evocation of both death and language, two poles around which the entirety of chapters 26 and 27 will continue to circle: "And after Christ shall have risen from the *dead* he shall show himself unto you, my children, and my beloved brethren; and the *words* which he shall speak unto you shall be the law which ye shall do" (verse 1, emphasis added). In the body of Christ we have both the death and the resurrection, along with an apparent reason for Christ's future visit to Nephi's descendants, namely, that they will receive Christ's words as their law. Against this backdrop, the deaths described in the following verses carry the connotative weight of the joint relationship between loss and recovery and their implicit link to the image of the emergent voice.

> And after the Messiah shall come there shall be signs given unto my people of his birth, and also of his death and resurrection; and great and terrible shall that day be unto the wicked, for they shall perish; and they perish because they cast out the prophets, and the saints, and stone them, and slay them; wherefore the cry of the blood of the saints shall ascend up to God from the ground against them. Wherefore, all those who are proud, and that do wickedly, the day that cometh shall burn them up, saith the Lord of Hosts, for they shall be as stubble. And they that kill the prophets, and the saints, the depths of the earth shall swallow them up, saith the Lord of Hosts; and mountains shall cover them, and whirlwinds shall carry them away, and buildings shall fall upon them and crush them to pieces and grind them to powder. And they shall be visited with thunderings, and lightnings, and earthquakes, and all manner of destructions, for the fire of the anger of the Lord shall be kindled

the very purpose of the readings in this project as experimental, hypothetical, and charitable, and given the absence of any specific textual evidence that Nephi did not equate authorship with ownership, I present this reading as an alternative, a possibility.

> against them, and they shall be as stubble, and the day that cometh shall consume them, saith the Lord of Hosts. (2 Nephi 26:3–6)

Notice the marked emphasis on equality in these verses. Everyone here will perish; death comes to all. The wicked will be destroyed due to their own destruction of the righteous prophets and saints. Beyond the act of death itself, Nephi's imagery depicts what might be called a persistent materialism surrounding death. The dead saints leave the physical trace of their blood upon the ground and the site of their burial that also holds the instruments of their deaths (perhaps the blood remains upon the stones themselves). The deaths of the wicked are also materially marked as the unrighteous are swallowed by the earth, covered by mountains, and crushed into powder by their own buildings. To die, here, is not simply to cease to exist, but to leave a trace of one's physicality upon or within the earth itself. Death, in other words, is here always the death of a *body*. The difference between the deaths of the righteous and the deaths of the wicked is also worth noting. When the righteous are slain, their bodies buried, and their blood spilt, their voice remains, the "cry of the blood of the saints [that] ascend[s] up to God from the ground" (verse 3). The wicked, however, are granted no such voice. Their destruction is complete, even to consumption. While the blood of the righteous retains its power to speak, the physical remnant of the wicked—the crushed pieces that are ground into powder—remains silent. This theme of speaking and silencing serves to flesh out of the connection observed between death and language in verse 1.

Nephi returns again to death and language later in chapter 26 in verses 15–17. This time, however, he interweaves his own voice with that of Isaiah (Isaiah 29:3–5). (Italicized material marks wording taken by Nephi from Isaiah 29.)[4]

4. For a more complete visual representation of the relationship between Isaiah 29 and Nephi's words here, please see appendixes 1–3.

> After my seed and the seed of my brethren shall have dwindled in unbelief, and shall have been smitten by the Gentiles; yea, *after the Lord God shall have camped against them round about, and shall have laid siege against them with a mount, and raised forts against them; and after they shall have been brought down low in the dust,* even that they are not, yet the words of the righteous shall be written, and the prayers of the faithful shall be heard, and all those who have dwindled in unbelief shall not be forgotten. *For those who shall be destroyed shall speak unto them out of the ground, and their speech shall be low out of the dust, and their voice shall be as one that hath a familiar spirit;* for the Lord God will give unto him power, that he may whisper concerning them, even as it were *out of the ground; and their speech shall whisper out of the dust.* For thus saith the Lord God: They shall write the things which shall be done among them, and they shall be written and sealed up in a book, and those who have dwindled in unbelief shall not have them, for they seek to destroy the things of God. (2 Nephi 16:15–17)

The imagery of death in these verses parallels that of the previous verses in several interesting and instructive ways. In the first part of verse 15, Nephi (through Isaiah's language) describes his distant descendants (note that he is speaking of the Lehites in the last days, well past the visit of Christ in 3 Nephi) as being "brought down low in the dust, even that they are not," an image that appears to parallel his previous description of the destruction of the wicked at the coming of Christ—they each are related to powder or dust, and they each are consumed past the point of existence, "even that they are not." The second half of verse 15 then returns to the issue of language, prophesying that the past words of the previously destroyed righteous and faithful saints will, following verse 16, be resurrected: they will rise up out of the ground, with the words emerging from the dust in a voice that will appear or be like that of a mystical séance—the necromancer who speaks with the dead.[5]

Death here, then, acts as a barrier, perhaps even a type of seal, that can be broken or penetrated by a most unusual figure: a wizard with his "familiar" who is given power, not by the devil or other unholy sources, but by God himself so that the wizard may "whisper concerning them." The wizard is not here to cast spells or to call forth the dead, but rather to act as the physical medium by which the voices of the dead may be brought forth out of the dust, out of death, and back into the discourse of the living. Notice that the wizard himself does not appear to have his own voice in this process—that is, his verbal production is entirely related to the words of the dead such that his own voice is, in a sense, voided or overwritten by the voices of the past. Unsurprisingly, these voices are returned to a material body through a reversal of the persistent materialism of death. As the voices are brought forth, they are reembodied within the *translation* of the book "written and sealed up" by the prophets of the past (verse 17). The wizard, of course, in this formulation, is associated with Joseph Smith Jr., and the text produced by this divinely aided encounter with the words of the dead is the Book of Mormon.[6]

While it may appear that Nephi's direct engagement with the themes of death and language ends here in chapter 26, I would argue that this is not the case. Chapter 27 opens with a return to the future historical content of Nephi's vision: the last days, the days in which the

---

5. This imagery, of course, derives from the original context and significance of "familiar" found in Isaiah 29. There the "familiar spirit" is understood in terms of the sorcerer's familiar, i.e., a spirit, often popularly conceived as having an animal form, that accompanies and attends the magician in his or her work.

6. In his role as prophet, seer, and revelator, Joseph Smith gave special attention to recovering and revealing records from the past—to providing the voices of the dead with bodies—throughout his life. As Samuel Brown explains in his *In Heaven As It Is on Earth: Joseph Smith and the Early Mormon Conquest of Death* (Oxford University Press, 2012), "Smith's inner circle clearly understood Smith's seerhood as a mode of revealing the records of the dead." Brown fleshes out Smith's role as a seer, arguing for seerhood as an active concern for voices past, demonstrated by bringing them into the present through the acts of translating, recording, transcribing, and writing, with the seer acting as a conduit for the dead.

Gentiles and the Jews will be "drunken with iniquity and all manner of abominations" (verse 1):

> *And all the nations that fight against Zion, and that distress her, shall be as a dream of a night vision; yea, it shall be unto them, even as unto a hungry man which dreameth, and behold he eateth but he awaketh and his soul is empty; or like unto a thirsty man which dreameth, and behold he drinketh but when he awaketh and behold he is faint, and his soul hath appetite; yea, even so shall the multitude of all the nations be that fight against Mount Zion.* For behold, all ye that doeth iniquity, *stay yourselves and wonder, for ye shall cry out, and cry; yea, ye shall be drunken but not with wine, ye shall stagger but not with strong drink. For behold, the Lord hath poured out upon you the spirit of deep sleep. For behold ye have closed your eyes, and ye have rejected the prophets; and your rulers, and the seers hath he covered because of your iniquity.* And it shall come to pass that the Lord God shall bring forth unto you the words of *a book*, and they shall be the words of them which have slumbered. (2 Nephi 27:3–6)[7]

The repetition of the motifs of both drunkenness and sleep throughout these verses is striking. The Gentiles and the Jews will be incapacitated as they fight against Zion; the Lord himself will inebriate them to the point of slumber. While technically living, in their drunken slumber the Gentiles and Jews call forth the image of the dead, silenced and immobile. In their examination of the text of Isaiah, where much of the language of these verses originates, modern critics note that in Isaiah, "Drink fends off but also anticipates death, anaesthetizing fear and rendering the subject unconscious."[8] While this interpretive precedent does not necessarily mean that Nephi himself uses the words

7. Italics indicate wording taken from Isaiah 29.

8. Francis Landy, "Tracing the Voice of the Other: Isaiah 28 and the Covenant with Death," in *The New Literary Criticism and the Hebrew Bible*, ed. J. Cheryl Exum and David J. A. Clines (London: Sheffield Academic Press, 1993), 150.

in this manner, it does not deny that possibility either. Therefore, we might argue that Nephi, through Isaiah's language, alludes back to the previous deaths of the unrighteous in a thematic gesture that then reinforces the reintroduction of the book containing "the words of them which have slumbered" (verse 6). At this point, the words breaking through "death" are not a cry for vengeance nor the whispering speech arising from the grave/ground, but the sealed words of those in the sleep of death, "those who have slumbered in the dust" (verse 9).

It should be clear by now that Nephi works and reworks the themes of death and textuality throughout chapters 26 and 27, and that the language of Isaiah 29 is essential to the formulation and expression of his thoughts. At this point, it finally becomes possible to ask with the appropriate force the question that interests me here: Why, if the Isaianic text is so crucial to his own formulations, does Nephi not alert us to Isaiah's authorship? Why are these words covered over by an undistinguished textuality that blurs authority and authorship?

Let us return to 26:16: "*For those who shall be destroyed shall speak unto them out of the ground, and their speech shall be low out of the dust, and their voice shall be as one that hath a familiar spirit;* for the Lord God will give unto him power, that he may whisper concerning them, *even as it were out of the ground; and their speech shall whisper out of the dust.*"[9] There are several readings of this verse yet to be explored that go beyond the thematic overview of death and language and point us toward a useful model for the Nephi/Isaiah textual relationship. To begin, it is worth observing that the phrase "one who hath a familiar spirit," drawn from Isaiah 29:4, is open to retranslation.[10] The Hebrew here can also be translated as "ghost-like." The same word is also used in 1 Samuel 28:8, where Saul asks a witch to conjure Samuel's spirit (or ghost) so that he may ask him for advice. A culturally and historically appropriate form of conjuration would be to first dig a hole in the ground and then pour a libation of wine into that hole so that the spirit could speak. Interestingly, the Hittite/Akkadian cognate of the Hebrew

9. Italics indicate wording taken from Isaiah 29.

10. Please note: I do not claim to be a scholar of Biblical Hebrew. This analysis arose during the seminar thanks to Julie Frederick's work on this section.

word can also literally mean a "hole in the ground." Therefore, another, somewhat strained but nonetheless possible translation for "one who hath a familiar spirit" would be "the hole in the ground (from which one conjures a ghost)." The necromantic themes here are also subtly linked to the idea of drunkenness through the libation of wine, which then, of course, propels us forward to the beginning of chapter 27 in which we have the Lord pouring out a spirit of deep sleep upon the *living*. While 26:16 presents us with the voice of the actually dead rising up out of the ground, whispering forth through the libation and bearing witness through the words of the book, 27:1–9 presents the living as zombies whose flesh lives but whose words are "as a dream of a night vision": unsubstantial, false, and ultimately unsatisfying.

It is also interesting to note that Nephi's words throughout these chapters display a consistent, if subtle, recontextualization of Isaiah's original discourse (another inverse relationship, perhaps).[11] If we examine Isaiah 29:4 in its original context, the state of speaking low out of the dust reads as a negative or undesired quality, yet in 2 Nephi 26:16, the tone is much more positive, in part due to Nephi's insertion of the figure given power by the Lord in order to bring forth the words of the dead. Beyond this insertion and the resulting shift in tone, the implied historical context of each verse is markedly different. Isaiah 29:4 describes the siege of Jerusalem during which the people are brought near death but do *not,* in fact, actually die. Isaiah's poetic imagery here implies that the people of Jerusalem will be *like* those who are dead; that they will be so weakened, and their voices so faint, that it will be *as if* their voices are rising from the grave. In 2 Nephi 26:16, however, the Lehites and their descendants really *are* dead. Nephi refers to two groups, each deceased: the latter-day Lehite descendants and the former authors of the book and their people. While Nephi uses Isaiah's language here—not only his imagery, but in terms of the actual construction of the passage itself, which contains word-for-word fragments citing 29:4—he is doing so in a particular way. Nephi is *not* quoting

---

11. I am indebted to discussion and comments by Kim Matheson and Grant and Heather Hardy during the seminar for the observations and thoughts developed in this section.

Isaiah. He is *not* bringing the hermeneutic and exegetical structures of Isaiah's words into his own words. Instead, he utilizes the shell or formal structure provided by Isaiah's sentences, but then gives them new life in the context of his own act of prophecy.

A pattern, at this point, begins to emerge. In a text that thematically addresses the physical death of a people and the later material resurrection of their voice via the text brought forth literally out of a hole in the ground, we also observe Nephi's own voiding (a type of death) and reappropriation (i.e., resurrection) of Isaiah's words. Nephi's explicit quotation of the so-called Isaiah chapters in 2 Nephi 12–24 demonstrates a desire to pass on the words of Isaiah *as* the words of Isaiah, clearly identified as such, to his descendants. Similarly, his careful explication of the themes of Isaiah 29 throughout 2 Nephi 25, although not a direct quotation, is accomplished in open acknowledgment as an act of summarizing Isaiah: "Now I, Nephi, do speak somewhat concerning the words which I have written, which have been spoken by the mouth of Isaiah" (2 Nephi 25:1). Implicit in this summary is the idea that Isaiah 2–14, with its historical specificity, is thematically reiterated by Isaiah himself in chapter 29. Each level of this summary, then, functions to reinforce the voice of Isaiah (rather than Nephi) in the ears and eyes of the reader of Nephi's text. In so doing, Nephi delineates a clear concept of authorship throughout both 2 Nephi 12–24 and 25: Isaiah is identified as the original author of the textual material presented in chapters 12–24 and the chapters are presented as direct quotations, carrying with them the authorial intentions, contexts, and even hermeneutic structures that originated with Isaiah himself. Chapter 25, while not authored by Isaiah, is again clearly marked by its own author (Nephi) as indebted to Isaiah's authorship. In summarizing his interpretation of Isaiah's message in chapter 25, Nephi alerts us to the fact that the words, while his own, are faithful to what he understands Isaiah's original intentions to have been. It is only after this Isaianic recapitulation that Nephi then turns himself toward his own project: to "proceed with my own prophecy, according to my plainness" (2 Nephi 25:7). Only after the words and themes of Isaiah have been put to rest does Nephi then continue on with his own work. Isaiah's words have, for Nephi, been presented, discussed, and, in this sense, fully experienced and, in opposition to the act of voiding, filled.

In part due to Nephi's prior careful replication and interpretation of Isaiah's words, his subsequent unattributed use of the language of Isaiah 29 in chapters 26 and 27 may be taken to be a deliberate move. It is imperative that we recognize the significance of Nephi's own authorial move here in chapters 26 and 27: he has just expended considerable energy copying, re-presenting, and interpreting Isaiah's words, and it is only after this act that he returns to his own acts of prophecy. And yet, his recent extended contact with Isaiah's words appears to have entered Nephi's own prophetic psyche on a linguistic level—Nephi finds himself unable to leave Isaiah's words, and yet, in order to remain faithful to his own prophetic calling and responsibility, he must break with Isaiah's authorial ownership over those words and find a way to appropriate them for his own prophetic task. How can Nephi wrest the writings of Isaiah 29 from their original context and authorship?[12] His decision to deliberately stop his previous pattern of attributing the quoted material to Isaiah marks a decision to accept his own authorial power and intention: Nephi may use the words of Isaiah in chapters 26 and 27, but he does so in a deliberate move of authorship that erases Isaiah's previous authorial identity and imprint upon the language. Returning to the central themes of these chapters, we see that the words of the dead emerge only after their corporeal demise. Death is the act through which the voices of the righteous are transfigured so that they may be brought forth as the words of the book, as scripture. Could it be that Nephi's relationship with Isaiah's *words* is ultimately, in a way, that of "the death of the author," famously articulated by Roland Barthes?[13] While I am fairly sure Barthes and Nephi would not appreciate the association, I find Nephi's linguistic movement here fascinating. Isaiah "lives" in Second Nephi, a formidable textual force that has stopped many an intrepid reader, only to ultimately "pass away" into Nephi's

12. Again, recalling that this particular reading under way is that of a modern reader, working with a modern notion of authorship.

13. See Roland Barthes, *Image—Music—Text,* trans. Stephen Heath (London: Flamingo, 1984), 142–48.

own prophecy. Nephi assumes his prophetic mantle and authorship through the symbolic killing of Isaiah as his (Isaiah's) words are buried beneath Nephi's recontextualization in order to meet Nephi's own prophetic necessities.

I realize this image—that of a prophet killing another prophet (whatever the sense and interpretive qualifiers of the term) in order to perform his own new and necessary act of prophecy—is problematic. But I also believe there are valid textual reasons to take this approach seriously and consider what it offers. To begin, Nephi's own autobiographic record is hardly empty of problematic moral images. Every reader of the Book of Mormon quickly arrives at 1 Nephi 4, in which Nephi recounts his decision to kill a temporarily incapacitated[14] Laban with his own sword and justifies his actions with the words of the Spirit: "Slay him, for the Lord hath delivered him into thy hands. . . . It is better that one man should perish than that a nation should dwindle and perish in unbelief" (1 Nephi 4:12–13). Laban's death, however sanctioned, is still a disturbing, problematic image. Why must Nephi kill Laban? In order to access the brass plates. What we have here, right at the beginning of the story of Nephi's own transition from son of a prophet to prophet in his own right,[15] is a narrative that relates the necessity of killing a man in order to bring into Nephi's possession the words of God.

If we have been reading carefully, Laban's death should not take us completely by surprise. When Lehi tells Nephi that he and his brothers

14. Given the previous discussion regarding the connections between the themes of death, drunkenness, and sleep, it seems not insignicant that Laban is found "fallen to the earth . . . drunken with wine" (1 Nephi 4:7).

15. In 1 Nephi, chapters 1–2, the prophetic activity and identity is clearly placed upon Lehi. It is only at the end of chapter 2, wherein Nephi speaks with the Lord, that we begin to see that prophetic mantle expand to include Nephi as well. The journey to Jerusalem to obtain the brass plates related in chapters 3–4 is significant to Nephi's development as a prophet because it is on this journey that he shifts from following behind his brothers (e.g., they cast lots initially to choose who will go talk to Laban rather than Nephi simply taking the lead) to testifying to them (see 1 Nephi 3:15–20; 4:1–4) and eventually to going on his own to obtain the plates (1 Nephi 4:4–6). When Nephi kills Laban, it marks the initiation of his prophetic pattern: he submits himself to the Spirit, follows promptings, and obtains the words of God.

must return to Jerusalem to obtain the brass plates, Nephi's initial response is one of obedience and action:

> I will go and do the things which the Lord hath commanded, for I know that the Lord giveth no commandments unto the children of men, save he shall prepare a way for them that they may accomplish the thing which he commandeth them. (1 Nephi 3:7)

These words are so familiar that we often miss their underlying echo of another voice of prophetic obedience:

> And he [Isaac] said, Behold the fire and the wood: but where is the lamb for a burnt offering? And Abraham said, My son, *God will provide* himself a lamb for a burnt offering. (Genesis 22:7–8, emphasis added)

The God who provides himself with a lamb for the offering is the same God who prepares ways for the obedient to fulfill His commandments. Nephi knows who it is that he has chosen to obey: he obeys the God of Abraham and of Isaac, participants in one of the most ethically problematic scenes in all scripture, that of a father commanded to sacrifice his son. But of course, their experience foreshadows the ultimate moral and ethical injustice, that of a God who sacrifices his innocent Son in order to provide a way to overcome death and damnation through the resurrection, salvation, and exaltation of the rest of his imperfect, sinning children. Christ does not die: he is killed. And the force of his charity and extent of his grace is felt more fully in part because we react to a killing rather than a death. What I find in these texts here is evidence that God utilizes our powerful moral and ethical reactions to killing in part in order to emphasize the importance of individual obedience, faith, and commitment to bring to pass the will of God.[16] It is this obedience, faith, and commitment—this

16. "Father, if thou be willing, remove this cup from me: nevertheless not my will, but thine, be done" (Luke 22:42).

charity—that I see at work in Nephi's textual relationship with Isaiah. When Nephi appropriates and recontextualizes Isaiah's words in 2 Nephi 26–27, he structurally reenacts the act that marked the beginning of his own prophetic identity—the killing of Laban—in a move that focuses the text toward the theological richness and prophetic power of Nephi's own writings that close out the remainder of 2 Nephi.

And yet, in light of the thematic structures we have recently examined, Nephi's authorial move here does not necessarily end simply with death. When we speak conversationally in the LDS Church regarding the supposed difficulty of the Isaiah chapters in 2 Nephi, we implicitly refer to Nephi's openly acknowledged citation of Isaiah 2–14 in 2 Nephi 12–24 and *not* to 2 Nephi 26–27. Ironically, Nephi's attributed citation of Isaiah is relatively straightforward, at least from a textual viewpoint, while the relationship between Isaiah 29 and 2 Nephi 26–27 complicates the text in a multitude of ways. As Nephi returns repeatedly to Isaiah 29, he does so from a new standpoint: that of a prophet uttering his own prophecy. The materials or words are textually reassembled in an act that calls up the image of creation—the unidentified or undifferentiated materials that are "organized" into a new earth—and Nephi as prophet thus secretly reanimates Isaiah, breathing new life into the dust of his words. Perhaps this interpretation gives us another way to read 2 Nephi 26:16: with Nephi himself occupying the wizard's role as he brings forth, through the power of God given to him, the words spoken by a righteous prophet who was destroyed, and whose voice then only spoke in whispers from the dust. The prophetic resurrection of Isaiah's words is not their (mere) repetition, but their reappropriation and recontextualization.

A final question: how do we react to Nephi's somewhat radical approach to authorship and prophecy? Are we ourselves under any obligation to imitate Nephi's actions? Surely not—the responsibilities of reading and interpretation as well as seeking continued revelation and prophesying do not weigh on each of us individually, do they?

And yet, in 2 Nephi 26:18 through 27:1 (a section in which Nephi stops utilizing Isaiah's language), there is an unsettling matter: Nephi turns to the theme of universalism. Verse 24 of chapter 26 presents us with a Christ who lays "down his own life that he may draw *all men* unto him" (emphasis added). In 26:28 we learn that the Lord does not command "any that they should not partake of his goodness. . . . *All men* are privileged the one like unto the other, and *none* are forbidden" (emphasis added). And 26:33 states most emphatically that the Lord "inviteth them *all* to come unto him and partake of his goodness; and he denieth *none* that come unto him, black and white, bond and free, male and female; and he remembereth the heathen; and *all* are alike unto God, both Jew and Gentile" (emphasis added). While the context of Nephi's discourse in this section of chapter 26 makes it clear that he sees this universalism as applying to the right and ability of every individual to receive the atonement, against our discussion of death and language another possibility emerges. If all truly are alike unto God, then the pattern here is clear. Nephi reads a scriptural text. He then shares those words and their interpretation with others. And finally, he takes it upon himself to make his own prophecy, weaving into his text as a voice whispering from the dust the words of Isaiah, together forming a new textual life. As we encounter the voices of the prophets in our scriptures, perhaps we are to do the same.

Seals, Symbols, and Sacred Texts: Sealing and the Book of Mormon

Julie A. P. Frederick

Second Nephi 27:7 tells us: "And it shall come to pass that the Lord God shall bring forth unto you the words of a book, and they shall be the words of them which have slumbered. And behold the book shall be sealed." When we picture the gold plates we may think of Arnold Friberg's painting of Moroni praying before burying the plates, or perhaps of one of several portrayals of Joseph Smith receiving the plates from Moroni. These images would perhaps remind us of Moroni's statement that he would "seal up" the plates (Moroni 10:2). Second Nephi 27:6–22 offers a prophecy of the coming forth of this sealed book. I would like to discuss in some detail what 2 Nephi 27 says about that seal, to evaluate what type of seal can fit Nephi's description, and to consider if and how that seal has any meaning for readers of the text of the Book of Mormon today.

As other papers in this volume make clear, 2 Nephi 27 is a prophecy written by Nephi in which he draws heavily on the text of Isaiah 29. In fact, most of Isaiah 29 is present in chapters 26 and 27 of Second Nephi, though Nephi adds significantly to the text and rearranges some of the verses from Isaiah 29.[1] Within this larger prophecy, 2 Nephi 27:6–22

1. See, in addition to the other essays making up the present collection, Robert A. Cloward, "Isaiah 29 and the Book of Mormon," in *Isaiah in the Book of Mormon*, ed. Donald W. Parry and John W. Welch (Provo, UT: FARMS, 1998), 191–247.

contains Nephi's specific prophecy of the coming forth of a book in the last days. The most famous passages of this section relate to the declaration of a learned man that he cannot read a sealed book, which was historically fulfilled by Martin Harris's visit to Charles Anthon.[2] Thorough studies have worked carefully through the historical documents relating to this visit, but because modern history does not bear immediately on the question of the seal mentioned in the same verses, I will not discuss such questions here.[3]

Instead I want to focus my attention on the many references to seals in verses 6–22, as well as on how those descriptions can enrich our understanding of the coming forth of the Book of Mormon. As will be seen, although the image of the seal suggests something quite material or physical, Nephi's employment of this image will consistently press us in the direction of the spiritual or the symbolic. Rather than presenting us, however, with simple symbols, Nephi's image of the seal provides the reader with a rich intersection of themes that have much to teach us about the meaning of the Book of Mormon.

Preliminarily, though, it should be noted that verses 7 and 10 make clear that more than one seal is under discussion in Nephi's prophecy. A first seal apparently seals the entire book (verse 7: "And behold the book shall be sealed"; verse 10: "the book shall be sealed by the power of God"). A second seal, however, seems to bind up only a part of the book, namely, the part that is *usually* referred to as the "sealed portion" of the plates. According to the text, "in the book shall be a revelation from God from the beginning of the world to the ending thereof" (verse 7), and this specific revelation has a seal of its own (verse 10:

---

2. A generally accepted reading of the specific fulfillment of this prophecy is as follows:

Verse 15: "him to whom [the Lord] shall deliver the book" (Joseph Smith)
Verse 15: "another" to whom the above delivers the words (Martin Harris)
Verse 15: "the learned" man who receives the words from "another" (Charles Anthon)
Verse 13: "a few" who view the book (the three witnesses)
Verse 14: "as many witnesses" (the eight witnesses)

3. See Brant A. Gardner, *Second Witness: Analytical and Contextual Commentary on the Book of Mormon,* 6 vols. (Salt Lake City: Greg Kofford Books, 2007), 2:381–93, for a discussion of how historical questions might bear on other aspects of the text.

"the revelation which was sealed shall be kept in the book"). Thus we have both a sealed *book* and a sealed *revelation* (the latter sealed independently of but contained within the former).

Some further preliminaries—primarily concerning the Hebrew behind Isaiah 29:11—need attention. Isaiah 29:11 introduces the metaphor on which Nephi so heavily draws: "the vision of all is become unto you as the words of a book that is sealed." This sentence is not itself present in Nephi's text, but it is nonetheless the origin of several other statements by Nephi. The Hebrew word in Isaiah 29:11 for "book" is *sfr,* a word that can mean scroll or document (and refers to any official or documented information). The word derives from a root that originally meant "to count" (in the sense of taking a census), coming later to mean "to account" or "to recount," that is, to write a history or a narrative.[4] The Hebrew word used in turn for "seal" in Isaiah 29:11 is *htn.* This verb means, straightforwardly, to seal a document, and the noun (*hotan*) derived from it can mean either a seal placed on a document or a signet-ring used to impress the seal.[5] Seals "both protected the integrity of the contents [of a document] and served to identify the sealer as author, witness, agent, buyer, or seller, depending on the contents and purpose of the text."[6] Importantly, in Isaiah 29:11 it is "the vision of all" that has become like an inaccessible document to Israel. The Hebrew phrase behind the KJV's "the vision of all" is *chzwt hkl,* a literal translation of which would be "the vision of the whole."[7] Although he omits this specific phrase from his direct quotation of Isaiah 29, Nephi does claim that "in the book shall be a revelation from God, from the beginning of the world to the ending thereof" (2 Nephi

---

4. Francis Brown, S. R. Driver, and Charles A. Briggs, *Hebrew and English Lexicon of the Old Testament* (New York: Oxford University Press, 1906), 706.

5. Ibid., 367–68.

6. Bonnie S. Magness-Gardiner, "Seals, Mesopotamian," in *Anchor Bible Dictionary,* ed. David Noel Freedman (New York: Doubleday, 1992), 5:1062.

7. See, for instance, Young's Literal Translation: "And the vision of the whole is to you," etc.

27:7). For Nephi, it seems, Isaiah's "vision of all" is to be likened to this "revelation from God."[8]

With these preliminaries out of the way, what can be said about the nature of the seals in Nephi's text? A first approach draws on the use of seals in Isaiah's Old World context, since it was from Isaiah that Nephi derived his discussion. In the Old Testament sealed scrolls are used for royal orders and official documents, such as deeds of sale and even marriages. Whatever method was used, the seal consisted of an impressionable substance (usually clay or wax) and the image impressed on it (usually by a stone, ring, or cylinder). The clay ensured that the document could not be accessed without leaving evidence of the tampering. Moreover, the impression on the clay provided authentication of the origin of the document. Examples of this type of sealed scroll can be found in various Old Testament texts.[9]

It should be noticed that the type of seal here under discussion is not a strong physical barrier. Anyone can break such a seal and access the writing supposedly protected within. But like seals on bottles of medicine today, these ancient seals were intended less to prevent physical access to the contents than to make clear that unauthorized access had

8. Note that revelations or visions "of the whole" are often written down and sealed up in scripture. Examples can be found in Daniel 12, Revelation 4–5, and Ether 3–6. Note in particular that Nephi himself knew of John's apocalypse. See 1 Nephi 14:27.

9. To take a couple: In 1 Kings 21, King Ahab desires to buy a vineyard the owner does not want to sell. Jezebel, the king's wife, therefore "wrote letters (*spr*) in Ahab's name, and sealed (*htn*) them with his seal (*htn*), and sent the letters unto the elders and to the nobles" (1 Kings 21:8). These letters effectively produced false witnesses against the owner so that he would be executed, making the vineyard available to Ahab. Such is the power of the seal. In another Old Testament text, this one from the book of Jeremiah, we find a detailed explanation of a property purchase: "And I bought the field of Hanameel my uncle's son, that was in Anathoth, and weighed him the money, even seventeen shekels of silver. And I subscribed the evidence, and sealed [*htn*] it, and took witnesses, and weighed him the money in the balances" (Jeremiah 32:9–10). After weighing the money, Jeremiah makes two copies of the purchase agreement. One he keeps, and the other one, the sealed copy of the deed of sale, is "put in an earthen vessel, that they may continue many days" (Jeremiah 32:14). Jeremiah's precautions demonstrate again the power of the seal. See also John W. Welch and Kelsey D. Lambert, "Two Ancient Roman Plates," *BYU Studies* 45/2 (2006): 54–76.

taken place. Just as the seal on a bottle of medicine today often reads, "Do not use if seal is broken," the seal on a document anciently could be said to say, "Do not trust the contents if seal is broken." The ancient seal, then, was more a symbolic than a physical barrier, a symbol of textual integrity and authority. For a document to be authentic, it had first to be sealed by authority and then transmitted without mishap to the correct recipient—the only one who was authorized to open the seal. Only then could the contents be revealed and accepted as authentic. Sealing a document in the Old Testament functioned in a way similar to notarizing a document today by authenticating its veracity.

As a metaphor, this type of seal would be appropriate for the gold plates ("the book") because they were (1) sealed by someone with authority (Moroni), (2) transferred without mishap to an intended individual (through the buried box), and (3) read by that authorized recipient (and him alone). Importantly, this *metaphorical* understanding of what Nephi describes as the seal on the gold plates as a whole *only* works as a metaphor: no literal impressed wax or clay seal is historically attested for the plates as a whole.

Other interpretive possibilities deserve mention. Occasionally, the Old Testament uses the phrase "sealed up" to mean "hidden" rather than "notarized" (though such usage never has reference to texts). Since in 2 Nephi 27:22 Nephi records the Lord's command to Joseph Smith that, after the work of translation was complete, he was to "seal up the book again, and hide it up unto me, that I may preserve the words which thou hast not read, until I shall see fit in mine own wisdom to reveal all things unto the children of men," at least part of the significance of the seal on the book is the hiddenness and silence that surrounded the plates.[10]

Another possibility can be derived from the Gospel of Matthew. After Jesus was laid in the sepulchre, some of the chief priests and Pharisees said to Pilate "Sir, we remember that that deceiver said, while

10. This is further substantiated by a statement on the title page of the Book of Mormon: the gold plates were "Written and sealed up, and hid up unto the Lord, that they might not be destroyed—To come forth by the gift and power of God unto the interpretation thereof—Sealed by the hand of Moroni, and hid up unto the Lord, to come forth in due time by way of the Gentile."

he was yet alive, After three days I will rise again. Command therefore that the sepulcher be made sure until the third day, lest his disciples come by night, and steal him away. . . . So they went, and made the sepulcher sure, *sealing* the stone and setting a watch" (Matthew 27:62–66, emphasis mine).[11] The idea in this text, clearly, is that someone trying to remove the body of Jesus would have to break the seal, thus leaving evidence of tampering. The seal was meant to serve as insurance against false claims of a miraculous resurrection; ironically, it eventually served as proof that the resurrection was not a deception. Like Jesus's body, the gold plates were placed in a stone receptacle covered by a rock. And, like Jesus's body, the plates were accessible only through divine means (the angel Moroni). It could thus be that the seal on the book discussed by Nephi is meant to be taken as proving that the gold plates were not part of a deception, since only divine figures could reveal the location of the plates.

As much as the first interpretive approach above, these last two possibilities remain appropriate to the gold plates only as metaphors.[12] Because each of the interpretive possibilities outlined so far deal with physical seals, they cannot make sense of moments in Nephi's prophecy like the instance of Martin Harris's explaining that he could not "bring the book" to Charles Anthon "for it is sealed" (2 Nephi 27:17).

Here let us turn to the second of the two seals Nephi describes, the seal described not as sealing the gold plates as a whole, but only sealing what Latter-day Saints commonly refer to as the "sealed portion" of the plates, the part of the record that Joseph Smith did not translate. The sealed portion is so named because there are documented,

---

11. Note that the stone laid on the lions' den in Daniel 6 was similarly sealed. Incidentally, both Matthew 27:63–65 and the Greek version of Daniel 6:17 use the Greek word *sphragizo* for "seal," which has many of the same connotations of authorizing and making inaccessible as its Hebrew counterpart. William Danker, ed., *A Greek-English Lexicon of the New Testament and Other Early Christian Literature* (Chicago: University of Chicago Press, 2001), 980.

12. Importantly, the image of the seal already functions in Isaiah 29 as a metaphor: the vision had become "*as* the words of a book that is sealed." If the seal set on the gold plates as described in 2 Nephi 27 must ultimately be regarded as metaphorical, it would mark Nephi's continuity with, rather than departure from, Isaiah.

modern claims that there was a seal on part of the plates. Joseph Smith himself stated: "These records were engraven on plates which had the appearance of gold, each plate was six inches wide and eight inches long . . . ; the volume was something near six inches in thickness, a part of which was sealed. The characters on the unsealed part were small, and beautifully engraved."[13] Sadly, this description does not tell us what the seal looked like, or even whether it was physical in nature, and other historical evidence is ambiguous. Because of the problematic evidence, Robert J. Matthews suggested that the sealed portion was removable from the rest of the plates.[14] Claims that the seal around the sealed portion was a metal band come from late interviews with David Whitmer. Brant Gardner, though, contends that no physical seal existed on either the gold plates or the sealed portion. He suspects that David Whitmer was remembering the stories about the plates rather than his own experience of them.[15]

Turning to what the Book of Mormon itself has to say on the subject, one finds references to the sealing of the plates in a number of

---

13. Joseph Smith, Jr., *History of the Church of Jesus Christ of Latter-day Saints,* ed. B. H. Roberts, 7 vols. (Salt Lake City: Deseret Book, 1971), 4:537. Note that this description was technically borrowed from Orson Pratt, who was presumably recounting what Joseph Smith had reported to him. See Orson Pratt, *A Interesting Account of Several Remarkable Visions and the Late Discovery of Ancient American Records* (Edinburgh: Ballantyne and Hughes, 1840).

14. Robert J. Matthews, *Selected Writings of Robert J. Matthews* (Salt Lake City: Deseret Book, 1999), 339. This would leave one wondering why, if the sealed portion were removable, Moroni would have given that part of the book to Joseph Smith at all. Note that while George Q. Cannon claimed that "about one-third" of the plates was sealed, Orson Pratt claimed that "about two-thirds" of the plates was sealed. Of course, neither of these men was a witness, nor did either of them explain where he obtained his information. See Daniel H. Ludlow, *A Companion to Your Study of the Book of Mormon* (Salt Lake City: Deseret Book, 1976), 320.

15. See Gardner, *Second Witness*, 6:218–24. As evidence against a physical seal, Gardner points out that though Emma Smith described rustling, through a cloth covering, the pages of the plates with her thumb, she said nothing of a non-rustleable part of the plates; and that neither the three nor the eight witnesses said anything about a sealed portion of the plates in their accounts of seeing and handling the plates.

texts.[16] In two of these (2 Nephi 27:22; Ether 5:1), Joseph Smith is told to not "touch" what is sealed. The emphasis here lies in the physical act of touching rather than the visual act of reading or even translating. This emphasis of the physical act suggests that there *was* a physical element to the seal on the sealed potion. In line with this, the most descriptive passages in the Book of Mormon about seals on the record are those that deal with the seal, which specifically seals the "sealed portion" (rather than on the gold plates as a whole). I would like to look at these passages carefully, turning only afterward to passages that deal with the seal on the gold plates as a whole, thus allowing insights from the latter texts to inform our reading of the former.

When the brother of Jared sealed up the record of his vision, he included two stones with it: "And behold, these two stones will I give unto thee, and ye shall seal them up also, with the things which ye shall write" (Ether 3:23). Moroni comments later that the Lord "commanded me that I [too] should seal them up; and he also hath commanded that I should seal up the interpretation thereof; wherefore I have sealed up the interpreters [the stones], according to the commandment of the Lord" (Ether 4:5). That the stones had to be sealed up along with the record suggests that the act of sealing the "sealed portion" was in some sense or at least in part physical. But in addition to the physical aspect of this seal, one detects in these passages a "linguistic" aspect: the *language* was, in addition to and like the physical part of the plates in question, sealed. Joseph received two stones (eventually called the Urim and Thummim) that were sealed up with the text, stones that he used for translating not the *sealed* portion (as was their stated intent) but the *unsealed* portion of the gold plates. Because the Urim and Thummim, at least in the beginning stages of translation, were necessary[17] to translate the unsealed part of the text, we can conclude that the same linguistic seal on the sealed

16. See 1 Nephi 14:26; 2 Nephi 26:17; 30:3; Ether 3:22–23, 27–28; 4:5; 5:1; Moroni 10:2.

17. Most historians conclude that Joseph Smith used the Urim and Thummim for the first stages of translation but then used the seer stone for the majority of the translation, especially after the loss of the 116 pages. See, for example, Matthew B. Brown, *Plates of Gold: The Book of Mormon Comes Forth* (American Fork, UT: Covenant Communications, 2003), 164–65.

portion also existed on the plates as a whole. Just as the text sealed by the brother of Jared was written in a language that could not be read because it had been (divinely) confounded (see Ether 3:21–24; cf. 1 Nephi 14:26), the gold plates were also written in a language that could not be read—not necessarily because the language had been confounded, but because the language did not exist anywhere else.

This linguistic seal is arguably also related to a "visual" seal: the plates remained "hid" from the world because Joseph Smith was commanded not to show them. The transcription of gold plates' characters taken by Martin Harris to Charles Anthon is described in 2 Nephi 27:15 as "these words which are not sealed." The transcription was not sealed (the transcribed characters of the unknown language were visually accessible), but, because Anthon could not translate the transcribed text, it seems that a linguistic seal of sorts remained in place. Even if Charles Anthon had had some familiarity with the language of the plates, being able to decipher characters is not the same as having authority to translate. To break the linguistic seal, a seer was needed, someone who would render the translation "a marvelous work" (2 Nephi 27:25) rather than an academic achievement.

Interestingly, 2 Nephi 27:1–5 describes the deplorable state of the world "in the last days, or in the days of the Gentiles" as being in part a consequence of a general rejection of "the prophets" and "the seers." I do not believe that the mention of prophets and seers in this passage—immediately preceding Nephi's description of the coming forth of the sealed book—is irrelevant or accidental. According to Mosiah 8:13, a seer is someone who has the ability to translate unknown languages. A seer is so named because of his or her ability to "see" what others cannot see.[18] Though not in 2 Nephi 27, Joseph Smith is called a seer in several other places in scripture, including 2 Nephi 3:6.[19] A large part of Joseph's role as a seer seems to have been to see what was sealed and "hid from the eyes of the world."

---

18. Another connection between the seer and the text that is lost on us in English is that the words *vision* and *seer* are cognates in Hebrew: to see a vision is to see a seeing.

19. See also D&C 21:1, 124:94, and 127:12 for Joseph Smith as a seer.

The linguistic and visual aspects of the seal—in addition to forcing us away from strictly physical questions in favor of more spiritual or metaphorical interpretations of Nephi's language—suggest to me a relationship between power with regard to language and righteousness.[20] Interestingly, the qualification for breaking the seals of the heavenly scroll in Revelation 4–5 is righteousness: after John sees the scroll and its seals, the angel asks, "Who is worthy to open the book, and to loose the seals thereof?" (Revelation 5:2), suggesting that only the righteous can have authority to open a text sealed by God. Significantly, 2 Nephi 27 portrays the unrighteous figure of the learned man as illegitimately claiming a kind of guardianship or mastery over language (2 Nephi 27:15: "the learned shall say: Bring hither the book, and I will read them").[21] The learned man in 2 Nephi 27 is thus like the scribes in the New Testament who "search the scriptures," thinking that "in them" they "have eternal life," but who are wrong because the scriptures "are they which testify of [Christ]" (John 5:39). The scribes believe that they have jurisdiction over the text, but it is Christ, not they, who teaches "as one having authority" (Matthew 7:29).

This discussion of seals in 2 Nephi 27 seems, in the end, to have come back to the question of authority, something I introduced early on, but only in a passing comment. I would like to conclude this study by looking briefly at how the question of authority, with regard to the seal, might deepen the meaning of Nephi's discussion. I might introduce this last, brief, somewhat speculative aspect of my discussion by noting simply that there is reason to explore the connection between

20. See Moses 6:5–7. Certainly, it is significant that God created all things either literally by speaking ("Let there be . . .") or through the Word—Jehovah. The power of God is unquestionably connected to language, and it would seem quite naturally to follow that only those with authority from God can exercise the use of language authoritatively.

21. The Hebrew for "learned" literally means "one who knows books" (*ydh sfr*). Thus Young's Literal Translation of Isaiah 29:11–12 reads: "And the vision of the whole is to you, As words of the sealed book, That they give unto one knowing books, Saying, 'Read this, we pray thee,' And he hath said, 'I am not able, for it [is] sealed;' And the book is given to him who hath not known books, Saying, 'Read this, we pray thee,' And he hath said, 'I have not known books.'"

sealing a text and the employment of what Latter-day Saints call the "sealing power" of the priesthood. But is such a connection justified?

In 2 Nephi 27:10, Nephi says that "the book shall be sealed *by the power of God.*" Interestingly, Nephi here seems to anticipate Joseph Smith, who explained in a letter that would become section 128 of the Doctrine and Covenants that the sealing power is a question first and foremost of *writing.* Describing the records that must be kept when the Saints undertake to create a "welding link of some kind or other between the fathers and the children" (D&C 128:18), Joseph claimed that the order of record producing and record keeping had been "prepared before the foundation of the world" (D&C 128:5). This order, he explains, was organized according to an

> ordinance [that] consists in the power of the priesthood, by the revelation of Jesus Christ, wherein it is granted that whatsoever you bind on earth shall be bound in heaven, and whatsoever you loose on earth shall be loosed in heaven. Or, in other words, taking a different view of the translation, whatsoever you record on earth shall be recorded in heaven, and whatsoever you do not record on earth shall not be recorded in heaven for out of the books shall your dead be judged. . . . And as are the records on the earth in relation to your dead, which are truly made out, so also are the records in heaven. This, therefore, is the sealing and binding power, and, in one sense of the word, the keys of the kingdom, which consist in the key of knowledge. (D&C 128:8, 14)[22]

One might, in light of this text, go so far as to suggest that the reason Joseph Smith was required to seal up the plates after translation (see 2 Nephi 27:22) was to return the Nephite record to its sealed status,

---

22. Note that the definition of the "sealing power" employed in this text is echoed in the Book of Mormon itself. See, for example, Helaman 10:7: "Behold, I give unto you power, that whatsoever ye shall seal on earth shall be sealed in heaven; and whatsoever ye shall loose on earth shall be loosed in heaven; and thus shall ye have power among this people."

allowing it to remain sealed in heaven, making it "a law on earth and in heaven" (D&C 128:9).

In the end, I would argue that what keeps so many people from taking the Book of Mormon seriously is not what it *says,* but the *the way* in which it says it—because of its claim to authority.[23] Joseph Smith's testimony at the beginning of the Book of Mormon makes an extraordinary claim about the origin of the book and the authenticity of the translation.[24] The (ancient) title page makes a similarly extraordinary claim about the authority of the book. These, along with the testimonies of the three and eight witnesses, serve as so many notarizizations of the book, asserting its genuineness and authenticity.[25]Whatever physical and spiritual seals have ultimately been placed on whatever parts of the gold plates, we are still faced with the reality that, in order to access the promises the book makes, we have to accept the possibility of its origin, authenticity, and authority. Only the believing can break the seals that keep the riches of the Book of Mormon "hid from the world."

---

23. See, for example, Terryl L. Givens, *The Book of Mormon: A Very Short Introduction* (New York: Oxford University Press, 2009), 4: "What the Book of Mormon claims to be is so radical that the storm of controversy over its origins and authenticity has almost completely obscured the book itself."

24. This suggests that Joseph Smith was himself the seal in question, that he *took the place of the seal* on the plates when Moroni delivered the plates to him. This interpretation can explain certain moments in Nephi's prophecy like the instance of Martin Harris's explaining that he could not "bring the book" to Charles Anthon "for it is sealed" (2 Nephi 27:17). Interestingly, the fact that the Book of Mormon text had to command Joseph Smith to "touch not the things which are sealed" seems to suggest that, had Joseph so desired, he *could* have had some kind of access to the sealed portion (see Mosiah 8:13). Perhaps Joseph Smith himself became the seal on the plates in that he made a promise not to touch what he could have touched had he chosen to do so.

25. It is noteworthy that verses 12–14 of 2 Nephi 27 clarify the role and purpose of the witnesses. Verse 12 explicitly states that "the eyes of none shall behold [the book] save it be that three witnesses shall behold it, by the power of God . . . and they shall testify to the truth of the book and the things therein." In verse 13 Nephi writes, "There is none other which shall view it, save it be a few according to the will of God to bear testimony of his word unto the children of men." In both descriptions, the witnesses are given visual access to the plates as well as acting as notaries verifying the truth and authority of the book.

And, still more demanding, if and when we receive a witness of the truthfulness of this book's claim, we in turn are called upon to become witnesses, to become ourselves, as it were, part of the seal that notarizes and testifies of the truth of the book. There where the symbol of authenticity, the authority of access, and the ability to interpret intersect, we can only hope that we, when the books are opened and the judgment is decided, shall be found.

On the Moral Risks of Reading Scripture

George Handley

READING SCRIPTURE in various religious cultures of the Book involves risk. If reading is posited as an encounter between the limited human understanding and the unlimited knowledge of God, faithful reading typically requires some kind of deference for the pure and transcendent meaning that the text purports to contain and healthy suspicion toward the impurities of human perception that might occlude such meaning. These impurities include our historicity (our embeddedness in time and space) and our partiality (our individual habits and proclivities of judgment that select and omit idiosyncratically in order to generate our interpretations of experience and texts alike). There is a rich history of the theology of reading within various religious traditions that has sought to understand the dynamics of this human contact with the divine word. It is not my purpose here to rehearse this history but to initiate a conversation, to essay a description of the inherent moral risks of reading implicit in a theology of restoration and continuing revelation. I do so in the hope of avoiding some of the common pitfalls of poor and superficial treatment of the question of what it means to read sacred literature. These pitfalls, I insist, are found on both sides of the polarized divide today between the ever-popular secular theories of culture and the often entrenched and defensive positions within religious cultures we find today.

Because the idea of a sacred text inevitably spinning off into infinite meanings, as many literary theories seem to suggest, is a problematic conclusion for believers, it is tempting to insist that a preestablished state of belief is enough to somehow transcend or avoid human dilutions or refractions of the truth. It is perhaps for this reason that believers often spend more religious energy attempting to help others work up the requisite state of belief than thinking about the potential for misunderstanding *within* a state of belief. Certainly one of the dangers of a believing reader is the confidence that what one understands is *necessarily* divine truth merely because of belief, as if belief alone guarantees the unadulterated truth, untouched by the stains of human perception. While such attitudes are not often fully articulated or defended, unfortunately they are often implicitly involved in the formation of belief. And while they are intended to respect the integrity of the sacred text, to the extent that they imagine the exchange between divine will and human understanding as static, they do not seek to account for remainders or gaps in reading. We enter an almost tautological cycle in which, because belief is required for understanding, understanding is identified as an understanding of truth only to the degree that it confirms that prior belief. Right reading here consists of the right belief emerging *before* the reading has even begun to take place; this risks implying, in other words, that reading is unnecessary since it produces nothing new. In this way, reading is imagined in such a way as to avoid the moral risk of judgment. Even a brief consideration of the political and sectarian dogmatism within many religious cultures today—and the concomitant neglect of the rich complexity of their own sacred texts—provides enough evidence that such reading theologies are alive and well.

The notion that belief precedes understanding stands opposed to the commonplace secular view of literature that has predominated in secular culture at least since Nietzsche's declaration of the death of God. In this view, judgment tends to take precedence over belief, and certainly over any notion of inspiration or revelation. According to Giles Gunn, in modern secular reading practices "one reinterprets for the sake of believing once again in the possibility of understanding and thereby rediscovers what it is like to believe."[1] Such attitudes respect the autonomy of the reader and her capacity to produce new understandings, while bypassing the problem posed by the possibility of divine intervention and communication of meaning. The implication, in other words, is that reading produces perpetually diversified meanings or "truths" that are merely idiosyncratic for each reader but never transcendent. Curiously here again, the reader evades moral risk since what is sought is merely an interpretation that holds a certain kind of creative integrity, persuasiveness, or style. Not surprisingly, we have seen over the course of the past century an increasing distance between these two positions, placing secular and sacred literature at greater and greater distance from one another because of the fundamental and mistaken assumption that they require irreconcilable reading strategies.

I wish to suggest that as a modern-day book of divine origin and translation, the Book of Mormon collapses this binary opposition between sacred and secular reading practices. It is a book of scripture that offers transcendent understanding in response to individual belief, but because the understanding that it offers reminds us constantly of the inevitability of remainders, it also offers grounds for belief in ultimacy. In its perpetual metatextual reminders about the inherent textuality of understanding, as well as the need for abridgment, revision, rephrasing, appropriation, and the seeming inevitability of anachronism (things that Nephi's use of Isaiah and other biblical language demonstrates particularly well), the Book of Mormon highlights the dynamic and incomplete nature of interpretation. In this sense, it raises the moral stakes—both the costs and the benefits—of reading, forcefully foregrounding both the need to bring ourselves fully to the text, rather than emptying ourselves of all prejudice and partiality, and the need to revise and to rethink what we thought we believed. The Book of Mormon demonstrates the paradox that no transcendent meaning can be gleaned from it without at least some individual wager of belief as to what it might mean. Indeed, all *transcendent* meaning appears to be dependent upon the bets of the *contingent* reader. It

1. Giles Gunn, *The Interpretation of Otherness: Literature, Religion, and the American Imagination* (New York: Oxford University Press, 1979), 47–48.

thus raises the moral stakes of reading to insist simultaneously on the divine and omniscient ultimacy that lies behind words to which we are answerable as well as on the need for creative, idiosyncratic readings that stem from the particulars and impurities of our historical and partial conditions as individual human readers. As the emblem of a theology of continual revelation, the Book of Mormon also sheds important light on the not-so-different processes of interpreting sacred and secular texts. In what follows, I wish to explore the theological implications of this process before then turning to a passage in 2 Nephi where we can identify these tensions.

Towards Mutuality

Matthew Arnold could never have argued for the inherent value of great works of literature in an environment that did not see texts themselves as primarily determinant of meaning. The very humanism he inherited from at least the Renaissance suggested that great books shape and mold great minds, great citizens, moral people. But in the West's disillusion with this "you-are-what-you-read" formula, we began to assume a Nietzschean responsibility to be more accountable for the worlds of our own making: it was not so much the text as the proactive creativity of the reader that could or should make meaning. In contemporary criticism, we are beginning to see a turn away from the polarizations implied in these two positions, coupled with a yearning for some way to reconcile these two (valid) views—a yearning that provides an opening for rethinking the nature of sacred literature.

Certainly, without attention to the ways that culture and worldviews shift through time, we become blind to the ways we want to read particular meanings into texts, and it is not difficult to see the danger in that. But without due attention to the text itself, we render all literature and all readings of equal value, something with which any believer in an authoritative text will inevitably feel uncomfortable. When this kind of radical flattening of the horizon of literary distinction occurs—between greater and lesser works of literature, between a poem, an essay, and a newspaper article, as we see in some forms of New Historicism or Reader Response Theory, for example—it also becomes virtually impossible to argue for the importance of the distinction between sacred and secular literature. And as I have suggested, one method believing readers have used to protect the text's authority is to assert that scripture itself assumes priority as determinant of its meaning and truthfulness, such that the truth of the word of God would seem to be self-contained and in no need of any reader's agency, historicity, or prejudice. If this attitude becomes excessive in its defensiveness, however, it begins to be intolerant of the ways in which the contingency of the human reader can become entangled or commingled with the will and mind of God. Human agency is assumed to contaminate and divert, perhaps even to pervert, the ways of God in the minds of men. And indeed, Peter, who warns that scripture is by definition not "of any private interpretation" (2 Peter 1:20),[2] also warns against the self-destruction of such misinterpretation. Speaking of Paul's epistles in 2 Peter 3, he notes:

> As also in all his epistles, speaking in them of these things; in which are some things hard to be understood, which they that are unlearned and unstable wrest, as they do also the other scriptures, unto their own destruction. Ye therefore, beloved, seeing ye know these things before, beware lest ye also, being led away with the error of the wicked, fall from your own steadfastness. But grow in grace, and in the knowledge of our Lord and Saviour Jesus Christ. To him be glory both now and for ever. Amen. (2 Peter 3:16–18)

Or as Alma simply says in the Book of Mormon, "Behold, the scriptures are before you; if ye will wrest them it shall be to your own destruction" (Alma 13:20).[3]

2. Note, of course, that the standard approach to 2 Peter 1:20 is heavy-handed. Commentators generally agree that the passage has reference to the prophet's interpretation of his or her revelatory experience, not to the reader's interpretation of scripture.

3. Note that to be learned, in these texts, is not to have profound knowledge of language, history, or exegetical prowess but to repent and submit oneself to grace and belief in Christ, so that proper understanding can be granted.

These are strong warnings. But, as my reading of 2 Nephi will show, they do not need to imply that we cannot bring our personality and invest it in the reading experience. If the refreshing and renewing power of new readers is disallowed, we may find ourselves leaning too heavily on the crutches of tradition and habit (and not, ironically, on the text), making ourselves vulnerable to assuming that language perpetually generates the same meanings across all times and places. We would, in other words, have to concede that human agency, imagination, and experience play no role whatsoever in the generation of divine meaning. While this would protect and keep unambiguously clear the boundaries between the human and the divine, such reliance on tradition actually bypasses rather than protects the special truthfulness of God's word. In order to preserve the notion of the text's special status above and beyond human stains, this approach holds to the promise of an absolute and transcendently correct reading, a mastery of the text. As Alan Jacobs argues, this position of mastery easily slides into a categorical suspicion of and freedom from the text and thus is not invested in the moral risks of reading. Though "freedom from' and 'mastery of' are related but not identical concepts," he points out, each entails "the elimination . . . of an ongoing dialogical encounter with the text, in which the reader and the text subject each other to scrutiny. . . . In neither case is there anything like real reverence, love, or friendship—in Bakhtin's term, *faithfulness* is lacking—and thus, in neither case is the readerly/critical experience productive of genuine knowledge (of the self or the other)."[4]

There is an essential moral weakness in the tendency to avoid confronting the human stains within sacred literature, just as there is in a hermeneutics of suspicion that distrusts its revelatory claims. In both cases, the reader is never required to take what Jacobs calls the "enormous risks" of using discernment.[5] In the former case, to assume a radical textual determinism is to assume that it is merely and always the text that produces meaning, never the reader. The inherent risk of engaging one's agency, choices, and judgment as a reader is bypassed in the interest of a meaning that is simply given, though how and why it is given or not

4. Alan Jacobs, *A Theology of Reading: The Hermeneutics of Love* (Boulder, CO: Westview Press, 2001), 70.

5. Ibid., 88.

given are rarely explained or are poorly theorized. Acts of interpretation in such a model are ultimately self-delusions, since the agency involved in discernment is ignored: a reader strictly intolerant of the ambiguities of human perceptions of divine will cannot explain how she avoids worshipping a god after her own image. In the case of a hermeneutics of suspicion, on the other hand, the determinism tends to lie with the reader who produces all meaning, the text being radically excluded from the process of meaning-making. The inherent risk of being answerable to an authority or a source of knowledge outside oneself is bypassed in the interest of a meaning that is simply chosen. Acts of interpretation in such a model are ultimately solipsistic illusions because the agency of discernment is the only agency at work: a reader strictly intolerant of the possibility of divine intervention and communication cannot explain how she avoids the false consciousness she originally sets out to escape.

There is, however, another possibility, one that seeks what the theologian Reinhold Niebuhr calls "mutuality."[6] Great knowledge comes at great risk—what Paul Ricoeur calls the very "wager" at the heart of all interpretation[7]—and one of the risks of reading scripture is to bet on one's interpretive capacity to discern the will of God. To have faith is to believe in the possibility that a mingling of human and divine understanding does not have to lead to deception even if it also means abdicating the need for absolute certainty. Faith maintains a margin of freedom from the text even as it seeks communion and understanding. Jacobs compares this mutuality to the dialogic imagination of Bakhtin, a kind of hope in a fruitful give-and-take between the reader and the text. He explains: "This hope involves neither *demand* nor *expectation*; indeed, if it demanded or expected it would not be hope."[8] Thus while "absolute suspicion—one that always and on principle refuses Ricoeur's wager—is the natural outworking of despair," its apparent opposite of "triumphalist confidence" (the "presumption" that one has apprehended truth that is always transcendently and eternally unchangeable) is also a form of "hopelessness."[9]

6. Ibid.
7. Ibid.
8. Ibid., 89, emphases in original.
9. Ibid.

I would suggest that the mutuality towards which Jacobs gestures can be heard in the Lord's chastisement in the first section of the Doctrine and Covenants. While the Lord criticizes those who "seek not the Lord to establish his righteousness" because every one of them "walketh in his own way, and after the image of his own god, whose image is in the likeness of the world, and whose substance is that of an idol" (D&C 1:16), we learn that it is precisely our human tendency to imagine gods and worlds of our own making that the Lord requires in order to reveal *his* will to us through his prophets, so that we might be corrected and gain wisdom. God's dilemma thus is that he must speak to his servants "in their weakness, after the manner of their language" (1:24). This mutuality of God's language and human language, between God's omniscience and our limited imagination, makes up the very structure of continuing revelation.

So what are the moral risks of reading scripture in this model of mutuality? We risk self-deluding idol worship—worshipping the god of our imagination—on one hand, and we risk self-exposure to the piercing eye of God on the other. The point is that there is no escape from these risks. We must be willing also to admit we have been wrong—wrong about God and wrong about ourselves. We must risk, in other words, the possibility of error because that is the only way that we might learn precisely where, in fact, we have erred. We generally do not take such risks unless we are willing to wager that such knowledge will change us, heal us, draw us closer to godliness. There is, on the one hand, error that leads to destruction, as Peter remarks, but there is, on the other, what the atonement makes of the errors we bring to the Lord: He turns the weaknesses and conditions of our human existence into the necessary stepping stones to and the strengths of our sanctification.

By asking us consistently to liken its pages to ourselves, as well as by consistently demonstrating through allegorical representation the risks and rewards of our interpretations, the Book of Mormon opens itself up perpetually to the contemporary moment of its reader. It makes actual its claims each and every time it is read. In this sense, for all its divinity, the Book of Mormon is also literally always secular—a word that indicates, among other things, that something is "in human time." The book, in other words, embodies the paradox that

God spoke and continues to speak "in human time," that prophets wrote and continue to write in human language, and that our reading practices cannot eschew—either through triumphalist confidence in received tradition or through secular despair in the face of the sacred—the inherent answerability and mutuality of the act of reading.

Symbolism and the Sacred

To this point in this paper, I have been speaking at a relatively abstract or theoretical level. Is there anything in scriptural texts themselves that justifies what I have outlined above regarding the nature of reading scripture? In the remainder of this essay, I would like to argue that there are, perhaps particularly in the Book of Mormon, consistent indications that reading scripture must take the kind of mutuality I have described as its aim. My argument, though, will not be that scripture makes an explicit claim about reading at the level of *content,* but rather that its very manner of inscription and internal organization implicitly gesture in the direction of a reading *process* of mutuality.

If we are to push the implications of the Doctrine and Covenants passage cited above, all forms of revelation in sacred literature are translations between divinity and humanity, and it is therefore no accident that we find in books that make special claims about points of contact between the human and the divine such a high level of figurative language, indirection, and self-reflexive metatextuality. Instead of signifying their fictionality, however, these symbols exhibit an inherent respect for and anticipation of the human reception of divine revelation that is built into the very structure of sacred texts. Thus, despite their didactic style and often declarative and imperative tense, scriptures also exhibit what Ricoeur calls their own "interpretive dynamism": "the text interprets before having been interpreted."[10]

This is an important feature of sacred texts that is often ignored by believing and nonbelieving readers alike. Figurative language implicitly,

---

10. Paul Ricoeur, "The Bible and the Imagination," in Paul Ricoeur, *Figuring the Sacred: Religion, Narrative, and Imagination,* trans. David Pellauer (Minneapolis: Fortress Press, 1995), 161.

if not explicitly, acknowledges the text's own partiality and its dependence on readers for the text to expand and magnify its meaning and thereby to work out its potential universality. Ricoeur points both to the sacred text's capacity to imagine its own poetic force and to the consequent need for a semiotic approach (as opposed to a "historical-critical method"). Understanding the truths of revelation is not so much a matter of contextual scholarship or even specialized exegesis, but a measured response to the guidance of the text's internally organized symbolism. Revelation, for Ricoeur, is thus the moment of transfer from the seemingly ahistorical space of a sacred meaning into our own history, something akin to what Nephi describes when he asks us to "liken" the scriptures to us. Readerly imagination displaces or relocates the text's meaning in the reader's capacity to imagine the figural nature of the text. Ricoeur explains: "A meaning potential in the language—that is, in the things already said—is liberated through the entangled twofold process of metaphorizing the narrative and narrativizing the metaphor."[11]

What Ricoeur describes here is a kind of dialogue between a dynamic, receptive, and changeable reader and a dynamic, receptive, and changeable text. Belief in the possibility of the former—which is belief in the possibility of repentance and of the atonement itself—necessitates belief in the latter.[12] Ricoeur insists, in other words, that if there is a readerly need to metaphorize the narrative of a sacred text, that need itself arises (as a response) from a semiotic pattern, already established within the text, that narrativizes metaphors. He takes as an example the parable of the sower, in which the "destiny of the sower is narrativized as the destiny of the word, [and] the destiny of the word is narrativized as the destiny of the sowing."[13] The sacred text, in other

---

11. Ibid., 159. Of course, there is no way to know for sure that one's wager on the meaningfulness of scriptural symbols will always bear fruit, but without the risk of feeling after this meaningfulness there can never be any corroborating response to the metatextual clues of the text. If we reject the wager because of intolerance for this ambiguity, it means that we accept that all declarations will merely and always be grounded in misreadings and that all literary forms are merely and always secular.

12. The perhaps ironic implication is that a fundamentalist notion of a sacred and unchanging, once-revealed Word is counterproductive, barring human change.

13. Ricoeur, "Bible and the Imagination," 159.

words, inserts "into the meaning of what is said something about its being said and its reception."[14]

If we were similarly to consider Lehi's journey into the wilderness, we would say that the story appears to have metaphorical shape, that it can be read as a metaphor for the mortal journey to the promised land of heaven. Certainly this is not an uncommon reading of the narrative, as we hear countless attempts—in talks, lessons, and sermons—to identify the Liahonas in our lives, the Lamans and Lemuels, the trials of broken bows, etc. What is striking in the narrative, however, is how often this metaphorizing—and this is to Ricoeur's point—is anticipated *in the narrative itself.* We see, for example, that the Book of Mormon is at pains to let us know that Lehi's stories and dreams are all told to us only secondhand by his son Nephi (whose recounting is inevitably mediated by his learning in the language of his fathers) and only after having passed through the editorial hand of Mormon—and we, of course, can only read these heavily mediated narratives in the translation provided by Joseph Smith. The book seems to insist rather emphatically on its textuality, making clear that reading, abridging, editing, and translating are integral components of being a seer who is also a translator.

But let us turn to a shorter, more specific text in order to illustrate this point more fully. Nephi's frequent and extensive borrowing from the language of Isaiah exemplifies the prophetic editorial work I have just described. The text tells us that Nephi is a close reader of texts but that he sees in the language of prophecy and revelation an opportunity to add likening layers of meaning that allow for multiple contexts and contingent readings that are still faithful to the mind and will of God. This is one of the Book of Mormon's most important and provocative ideas, and it implicitly suggests that faithful reading should be generous, aware but forgiving of human stains and weakness in the work of giving new life to the otherwise dead letter, just as God appears to be willing and able to use the same limited human language across a variety of contexts without compromising his truths. In fact, the implication seems to be that God's transcendent and revealed meaning

14. Ibid., 158.

actually *depends on* multiple readings in order to reveal the fullness of his truth, which is to say that the truth depends on human imagination, one reader at a time. Seeing multiple applications for the same passages of scripture to radically distinct moments in human history, Nephi encourages us to do the same.

In perhaps one of the most important instances of Nephi's approach to Isaiah, we see in 2 Nephi 27 a citation of verses from Isaiah 29 alluding to a sealed book that cannot be read. That the passage appears to be a prophecy of our time would seem to be the reason for its citation, but it comes to us as such only because it is, as presented in the text, already interpreted by Nephi. Nephi's editorial work here is a reading we are asked to model, and it is a perfect example of what Ricoeur means by suggesting that we should metaphorize narrative (creatively read 2 Nephi 27), which is already a narrativized metaphor (2 Nephi 27 being already a creative reading of Isaiah 29). When we are told that this book contains the words of "those who have slumbered in the dust" and that they shall be delivered "unto another" (27:9), we are presented with a reference to the words of the dead that are, among other possibilities, an emblem of the book—the Book of Mormon—in our hands.

Of course we know that this is a prophecy of the Book of Mormon at least because of the Charles Anthon incident. It would be a narrow reading, however, to see it only as a prophecy of this particular incident and therefore only as a prophecy about the Book of Mormon. Admittedly, the language of the prophecy points us in this direction. Note, for example, just how much more detail is provided in Nephi's version of Isaiah's text than in the Bible, detail that seems clearly intended to secure the connection with the Anthon incident. But Nephi expands on the story enough to go through specification to a kind of generalization. For example, verse 6 establishes simply that the Lord will bring forth unto his addressee ("unto you") the words of a book that will come from them who have slumbered. But Nephi appears to be addressing the remnant of the house of Israel as well as all people everywhere, especially those who have "closed [their] eyes" and rejected the prophets because of iniquity. So it is a historically specific people of the covenant he addresses (the remnant of the house of Israel),[15] but also apparently any generic reader whatsoever.[16] Thus, even as he adds details to Isaiah's text in order to secure a connection between the prophecy of Isaiah and the Anthon incident, Nephi himself begins to allegorize that latter-day incident, providing the beginnings of its universalization.

Importantly, Nephi's implicit allegorization of the Anthon incident is anticipated in the allegorizing language of Isaiah himself. Note that Isaiah speaks allegorically when he says: "The vision of all is become unto you *as* a book that is sealed." And it is this *as* into which Nephi inserts his own creative appropriation of Isaiah 29. And Nephi's explanations, the context of nineteenth-century experience, and our own contemporary perspective would seem to complete the allegory: the rejection of the authenticated translation by a learned man is an allegory of the wisdom of the world more generally and its rejection of revelation—a mistake we must not make. Going still further, though, one can take as allegorical also the sacred book in 2 Nephi 27, understanding it as an emblem of a history—*any* history—that is lost to us until sufficient repentance has taken place. The reader, on this approach, is implied to be someone always awaiting the further opening of a sealed book. Indeed, because the Book of Mormon itself makes note of its own sealed and lost portions and makes claims about other records waiting to come forth until all revelations (i.e., Isaiah's "vision of all" or Nephi's "revelation from God, from the beginning of the world to the ending thereof") are finally read, it (the Book of Mormon itself) can only serve as an intermediate step, a stepping stone, as it were, toward a greater understanding of God's revelations. Even as it reveals, the book in Isaiah's/Nephi's prophecy keeps us aware of the still-slumbering dead, of ourselves as perhaps the still-slumbering reader, and of every sealed book still awaiting further translation.

---

15. This is indicated in the footnote to Mormon 5:12 that is found in the 1981 edition of the Book of Mormon.

16. This is surmised from his opening address in this chapter to the Jews and the Gentiles and to "those who shall be upon other lands, yea, even upon all lands of the earth" (27:1).

Verses 10 and 11, moreover, seem to clarify the distinction between two kinds of sealed books and aid us in understanding this idea. One book is sealed because of pride, wickedness, wisdom of the world. This is the portion of the book described as given to "another,"[17] but it is distinct from the sealed book that holds "all things from the foundation of the world unto the end thereof." One way of understanding this might be to suggest that there is wickedness that prevents some from accepting the divinity of the Book of Mormon, and there is wickedness endemic to the human condition as such that prevents all of us—even those who accept the Book of Mormon—from being ready to "read by the power of Christ" to the point that "all things shall be revealed until the children of men, which ever have been among the children of men." Can we assume that as long as history remains a mystery to us—as long as all we can produce is fragmented knowledge—it is a sign that we remain in this general state of insufficient grace to be able to read the meaning of all things? Certainly, we are here implicitly enjoined to retain hope and resist both the temptations of secular chauvinism and of the believer's triumphalist confidence that Nephi chastises in later chapters when he complains of those who proclaim, "All is well—we have a Bible!"[18]

Verse 12 adds an interesting twist to all this. The verse declares that when the book is delivered to "the man of whom I have spoken" (surely Joseph Smith), "the book shall be hid from the eyes of the world." Such hiding was earlier spoken of in somewhat more allegorical terms (the slumbering, blind, and dreaming wicked who cannot understand God's revelations), but here it seems both allegorical *and* literal: "the eyes of none shall behold it save it be that three witnesses shall behold it." What seems especially rich about this figural and literal blindness, this figural and literal revelation, is that it posits the possibility that the very dichotomy between figural and literal is false. A refusal to read a sealed book, on the one hand, is here contrasted with the blessing of seeing the physical plates. The former position is based on faith in rationalism to the point that it refuses empirical evidence, the latter

17. The footnote for verse 10 in the 1981 edition of the Book of Mormon sends the reader to Joseph Smith–History 1:65, the story of the Anthon incident.

18. See 2 Nephi 28:21, 25; 29:3–13.

on faith in revelation to the point that it is rewarded with empirical evidence. The authentication of the translation, in other words, will not come from worldly wisdom but from, of all things, empirical experience, albeit facilitated and supplemented "by the power of God." The Book of Mormon, although suggestive of God's many mysteries, is not shrouded in mysticism. It is a book that promises revelation and delivers on its promise to those willing to make the wager. Unwillingness leads to our own condemnation—the only and very important caveat being that we should be careful not to overstate what we know, since the book in our hands is a metonym of the great book recording all things from the foundation of the world, a book that remains at least partially if not still substantially sealed.

Thus the sealed book in Isaiah becomes a prophecy about something much more fundamental and widely applicable than just an instantiation of the Book of Mormon's historicity and truthfulness. It is a prophecy about prophecy, a revelation about revelation, and it reaches from the beginning to the end of time. The sealed book is an emblem of the very language and knowledge of God and of our relationship to the hope we may or may not have in God's capacity to reveal all things to us. This would suggest that obtaining the power to revive the meaning of the words of the dead requires something from the reader: a purification of the heart, a point verse 12 makes most emphatically. Such purification does not happen, though, without our wagering on the possibility that a sealed book can speak, nor without risking the possibility that what it speaks might reveal the fullness of our sins and wickedness. No one wants to open such a Pandora's box without the hope that such knowledge will cleanse and purify: it *only* damns the one unwilling to believe it can be read or, as it were, unsealed. The sealed book in Isaiah and Nephi is therefore an emblem of hope in our potential, ultimately, to know all things, to obtain the mind of God. In this sense, it is also a warning of what we stand to lose when we assume the "learned" arrogance of a hermeneutics of suspicion, or when we assume the triumphalist confidence that we have all that we need, that we have indeed already taken possession of the mind of God by virtue of having obtained a fundamental knowledge of his revelations.

Ricoeur insists that a "a theology that confronts the inevitability of the divine plan with the refractory nature of human actions and passions is a theology that engenders narrative."[19] Surely a theology like ours that produces texts and narratives in excess of the Bible is guilty as charged: it insists on this meeting ground between a divine plan and the unpredictable and potentially chaotic nature of multiple, individual interpretations. Consistent, then, with the fundamental meaning of a God in mortal flesh, it insists that the sacred is an encounter between the will of God and the will of men, the language of God and the language of men, heaven and earth, spirit and body. In so doing, our theology perpetually produces texts that, in their overt textuality, suggest their own nature as palimpsests and therefore point to the need for the poetic imagination of readers and for the unending need for more readers to come. What in other words keeps scripture alive and dynamic and from becoming flattened out by the exercises of tradition is the vivification of new interpretations, which is another way of saying that what makes the gospel true is its relevance to human narratives, seized upon by one reader at a time.

Rising to the challenge of reading revealed words seems, in a word, to begin with a paradoxical recognition of the fact of the Lord's having withheld the fullness of revelation from us, of the fact that what we are reading in scripture is always partial, incomplete, and stained by human weakness. This opens up for the reader a choice: either I want to know all things, *even if it means I must confess that I have erred and will continue to err in my quest to love God and gain His knowledge*; or I do not want to know all things, *even if it means that in my fear I err.* It is a choice literally between life and death. We are broken, wayward humans, either way. But the hope in Christ is hope in a translation that miraculously places the will and mind of God in human flesh and posits the hope of such dead flesh finally conforming to the life-giving will and mind of God, a resurrection of the mind, as it were. To read scripture in faith is, in the end, to believe in the possibility that all of our broken readings might somehow be made whole once all the pages of the sealed book have finally been opened.

19. Ricoeur, "The Bible and the Imagination," 182.

Works of Darkness: Secret Combinations and Covenant Displacement in the Book of Mormon

Kimberly M. Berkey

WHILE THE SMALL PLATES' AWARENESS of their own latter-day emergence—as a component part of the Book of Mormon—is fairly well recognized, it has not yet been systematically traced through the entire record. Less well known is the Book of Mormon's deep awareness of secret combinations and the risk they pose specifically to the covenant. By tracing the theology of the Lehitic covenant through the record and closely examining the editorial process surrounding Helaman 5, this paper will deal thematically with both concerns as a method of pointing out the Book of Mormon's main purposes from the point of view of its ancient authors/editors—namely, that the Book of Mormon is intended to warn the Gentiles about secret combinations in order to ensure the fulfillment of the Lehitic covenant.

I should begin with a short discussion of terminology, particularly regarding what I mean by the "Lehitic covenant." This covenant, as I understand it, encompasses all the prophecies concerning Lehi's posterity, and it includes four basic elements: (1) settlement in a promised land (2 Nephi 1:5); (2) the familiar assurance that "inasmuch as ye shall keep my commandments ye shall prosper in the land" (Jarom 1:9); (3) a guarantee that Lehi's seed will never perish (2 Nephi 25:21); and (4) the promise that a record will come forth to bring the remnant of Lehi's seed to the knowledge of the covenant. It is this last element in particular that concerns us here. Thus with the term *covenant displacement* I refer to the idea that, at any given point, the complete fulfillment of these several elements of the covenant remains postponed—and in particular that the Lehitic covenant holds force past the end of the Book of Mormon and persists today, its fulfillment still to come.

The small plates of the Book of Mormon are keenly aware of their own emergence in the latter days and make frequent reference to this fourth element of the Lehitic covenant. The title page of the Book of Mormon points to this textual self-consciousness when it qualifies the Lamanites as "a remnant of the house of Israel" and addresses the record to them, "to show unto [them] what great things the Lord hath done for their fathers; and that they may know the covenants of the Lord, that they are not cast off forever." Second Nephi 30:3 makes a similar point: "After the book of which I have spoken shall come forth, and be written unto the Gentiles, and sealed up again unto the Lord, there shall be many which shall believe the words which are written; and they shall carry them forth unto the remnant of our seed." Later writers were also aware of this prophecy. Says Enos: "I did cry unto God that he would preserve the records; and he covenanted with me that he would bring them forth unto the Lamanites in his own due time" (Enos 1:16).

Second Nephi 26–27 encapsulates this focus, speaking at great length about the coming forth of the Book of Mormon. In these chapters, Nephi reworks the text of Isaiah 29, weaving it with his own prophecy. Less well known is the fact that he also alludes to the sermon of his brother Jacob from 2 Nephi 6–10.[1] A number of identical phrases are found in both chapters.[2] What is more, Nephi elaborates on a theme introduced

1. For this information and the evidences that follow, I am indebted to Heather and Grant Hardy, who introduced it during the course of the online collaboration of the seminar.

2. "He that fighteth against Zion shall perish" (2 Nephi 10:13, 16; 26:30–31); "I will be a light unto them" (2 Nephi 10:13; 26:29); "secret works of darkness and murders" (2 Nephi 10:15; 26:20); and "both Jew and Gentile, both bond and free, both male and female" (2 Nephi 10:16; 26:33).

by Jacob: that the Gentiles are a means of God's judgment on Israel but will also be the means of Israel's ultimate salvation. Nephi thus ensures that each of the "three witnesses" of the small plates—Nephi, Jacob, and Isaiah—contributes to the message of these two chapters, particularly as they relate to the redemption of Israel through the emergence of the Book of Mormon. In addition to discussing the redemption of Israel, each of these three witnesses, in the chapters Nephi incorporates, makes mention of secret combinations. Importantly, the phrase *secret combinations* is found only twice in all of the small plates—once in 2 Nephi 9:9 and again in 2 Nephi 26:22. Jacob makes it clear that the author of these covert organizations is none other than the devil: "[The] devil . . . stirreth up the children of men unto secret combinations of murder and all manner of secret works of darkness" (2 Nephi 9:9). Nephi, in nearly identical terms, writes, "There are also secret combinations, even as in times of old, according to the combinations of the devil, for he is the founder of all these things; yea, the founder of murder, and works of darkness" (2 Nephi 26:22). Not to be left out, Isaiah describes those who "seek deep to hide their counsel from the Lord, and their works are in the dark, and they say, Who seeth us? And who knoweth us?" (2 Nephi 27:27; cf. Isaiah 29:15).

Nephi has chosen his sources wisely. His Isaianic midrash is performed on a chapter that combines the theme of secret combinations with the coming forth of a sealed book, and his allusion to the words of his brother Jacob incorporates the only other location in the small plates where secret combinations as such are explicitly mentioned. Nephi's encapsulation of the self-conscious meta-text of the small plates is inseparable from the question of secret combinations.

Such insights allow for an analysis of the broad structure of 2 Nephi 26–27. These chapters are organized around the histories of two groups of people: the Lehites and the Gentiles. Verses 1–18 of chapter 26 concern Lehi's seed. Signs of Christ's death and resurrection are given, followed by a brief interim of righteousness, succeeded by rapid moral decay and the complete destruction of the Nephites. It is in the midst of this turmoil, besieged by the Lord God, "brought low in the dust," that a record is "written and sealed up in a book." With this, Nephi turns to the question of the Gentiles in 2 Nephi 26:19–27:33. Secret combinations are mentioned first (26:22), after which there is a lengthy aside contrasting the works of darkness with the Lord's pattern of inclusion and light (26:22–33). As with the Lehites, the text goes on (27:1–24) to describe a destruction that shares many of the same elements with the Nephites' extermination (thunder, earthquakes, fire), and it culminates in the coming forth of the record—including the prophecy traditionally interpreted as a specific reference to Professor Charles Anthon.[3] The prophecy comes to its climax with a direct quotation from the Lord (27:25–35), who announces that he is "able to do [his] own work," pronounces woe on secret combinations, and effects a series of reversals (the deaf shall hear, the blind see, the poor rejoice, and those who erred come to understanding).

Nephi structures history around two separate, but parallel, events, each involving a destruction and the record. For the Lehites it is a question of *writing* the record, while for the Gentiles it is the *coming forth* of that same record, but both events hinge on a question of destruction and how that destruction will affect the book in question. For the Nephites, it is destruction that necessitates the record's creation; for the Gentiles, final destruction is averted by the record's reemergence.

---

3. For examples, see Brant A. Gardner, *Second Witness: Analytical and Contextual Commentary on the Book of Mormon* (Salt Lake City: Greg Kofford Books, 2007), 2:382, 385–91. Ed J. Pinegar and Richard J. Allen, *Commentaries and Insights on the Book of Mormon: 1 Nephi–Alma 29* (American Fork, UT: Covenant Communications, 2007), 222–24. George Reynolds and Janne M. Sjodahl, *Commentary on the Book of Mormon* (Salt Lake City: Deseret Book, 1955–61), 1:396. Joseph Fielding McConkie and Robert L. Millet, *Doctrinal Commentary on the Book of Mormon* (Salt Lake City: Deseret Book, 1987), 1:320–23. Monte S. Nyman, *I, Nephi, Wrote This Record: A Teaching Commentary on the First Book of Nephi and the Second Book of Nephi* (Orem, UT: Granite Publishing, 2003), 659. Robert A. Cloward, "Isaiah 29 and the Book of Mormon," in *Isaiah in the Book of Mormon,* ed. Donald W. Parry and John W. Welch (Provo, UT: FARMS, 1988), 223–26. Among these, only S. Michael Wilcox attempts to read the passage as allegorical, and only after first attesting the Charles Anthon interpretation, in "Nephi, Isaiah, and the Latter-day Restoration," in *The Book of Mormon: Second Nephi, the Doctrinal Structure,* ed. Monte S. Nyman and Charles D. Tate Jr. (Provo, UT: Religious Studies Center, Brigham Young University, 1989), 236–37.

Mormon and Moroni as Editors

Mormon and Moroni, the primary editors of the Book of Mormon, seem to have been profoundly influenced by 2 Nephi 26–27. This can be witnessed especially through a series of similarities between 2 Nephi 26–27 and Mormon 8, laid out in table 1 below.[4]

If this table assembles primarily thematic resemblances between 2 Nephi 26–27 and Mormon 8, it overlooks one further similarity between Nephi and Mormon/Moroni: a turn to the future.[5] This is particularly relevant in terms of something I will call covenant displacement. A temporal gap is evidenced in the division of 2 Nephi 26–27 as outlined above. The second half of these chapters (2 Nephi 26:19–27:33) looks ahead to the role of the Gentiles, emphasizing the fulfillment of the Lehitic covenant in their day, completely disregarding the two-thousand-year-long separation between that fulfillment and the very nation to whom the covenant owes its name. Mormon and Moroni likewise show a heavy preoccupation with the future readers of their record, going so far as to leave off writing narrative in order to address the Gentiles directly (see Mormon 5:22–24; Ether 8:23–24; Moroni 10). This strong orientation to future readers—Mormon's and Moroni's as much as Nephi's—is a

4. Mormon 8 is a fascinating confluence of editorial intentionality. It marks the beginning of Moroni's first contribution to the Book of Mormon after the death of his father, which demonstrates a concerted effort to include the letters and prophecies of Mormon, perhaps as a posthumous get-to-know-you of the man responsible for much of the Book of Mormon. That Moroni uses his position as narrator to resurrect the voice of Mormon creates a truly unique textual relationship between father and son.

5. This point has recently been recognized by Grant Hardy as well. See Grant Hardy, *Understanding the Book of Mormon: A Reader's Guide* (New York: Oxford, 2010), 78–79, 82, 94. German scholar Gerhard von Rad finds this orientation to the future in Isaiah, as well: "It is at this point, the passionate elimination of all reliance on oneself, that Isaiah's zeal begins. That he saw a great act of deliverance lying in the immediate future was only one side of his message. . . . The 'object' upon which this faith should be based did not, however, as yet exist for his contemporaries; it lay in the future. The astonishing thing was therefore this: Isaiah demanded of his contemporaries that they should now make their existence rest on a future action of God. . . . If his own generation had rejected it, then it must be put in writing for a future one" (*Old Testament Theology*, trans. D. G. M. Stalker, 2 vols. [New York: Harper and Row Publishes, 1965], 2:160–67).

Table 1. Comparing Nephi and Moroni

	2 Nephi 26–27	Mormon 8
Isaiah	(Midrash on Isaiah 29)	"Search the prophecies of Isaiah" (Mormon 8:23)
Voices from Dust	"For those who shall be destroyed shall speak unto them out of the ground, and their speech shall be low out of the dust" (2 Nephi 26:16)	"Those saints who have gone before me . . . shall cry, yea, even from the dust will they cry unto the Lord" (Mormon 8:23)
Speak from Dead	". . . and their voice shall be as one that hath a familiar spirit" (2 Nephi 26:16)	"And it shall come even as if one should speak from the dead" (Mormon 8:26)
Blood from Ground	"The cry of the blood of the saints shall ascend up to God from the ground against them" (2 Nephi 26:3)	"The blood of the saints shall cry unto the Lord" (Mormon 8:27) "The blood of their fathers and their husbands . . . cry unto the Lord from the ground" (Mormon 8:40)
Destruction	"They shall be visited with thunderings, and lightnings, and earthquakes and all manner of destructions, for the fire of the anger of the Lord shall be kindled against them, and they shall be as stubble" (2 Nephi 26:6) "They shall be visited of the Lord . . . with thunder and with earthquake, and with a great noise, and with storm, and with tempest, and with the flame of devouring fire" (2 Nephi 27:2)	"There shall be heard of fires, and tempests, and vapors of smoke in foreign lands; and there shall also be heard of wars, rumors of wars, and earthquakes in divers places" (Mormon 8:29–30)
Opposition	"Those who have dwindled in unbelief shall not have them, for they seek to destroy the things of God" (2 Nephi 26:17)	"He that . . . shall say: We will destroy the work of the Lord, and the Lord will not remember his covenant which he hath made unto the house of Israel—the same is in danger to be hewn down and cast into the fire" (Mormon 8:21)

	2 Nephi 26–27	Mormon 8
Wealth	"The laborer in Zion shall labor for Zion; for if they labor for money they shall perish" (2 Nephi 26:31)	". . . lift themselves up in the pride of their hearts, unto the wearing of very fine apparel. . . . For behold, ye do love money, and your substance, and your fine apparel" (Mormon 8:36–37)
Priestcraft	". . . preach up unto themselves their own wisdom and their own learning, that they may get gain" (2 Nephi 26:20) "He commandeth that there shall be no priestcrafts; for, behold, priestcrafts are that men set themselves up for a light unto the world, that they may get gain and praise of the world; but they seek not the welfare of Zion" (2 Nephi 26:29)	"There shall be churches built up that shall say: Come unto me, and for your money you shall be forgiven of your sins" (Mormon 8:32) "Leaders of churches and teachers shall rise in the pride of their hearts" (Mormon 8:28) ". . . because of the praise of the world" (Mormon 8:38)
Many Churches	". . . have built up many churches" (2 Nephi 26:20) "There are many churches built up which cause envyings, and strifes, and malice" (2 Nephi 26:21)	"There shall be churches built up" (Mormon 8:32)
Sign-Seekers	"And the learned shall say: Bring hither the book, and I will read them" (2 Nephi 27:15)	"And he that saith: Show unto me, or ye shall be smitten—let him beware lest he commandeth that which is forbidden of the Lord" (Mormon 8:18)
Secret Combinations	"And there are also secret combinations, even as in times of old, according to the combinations of the devil" (2 Nephi 26:22) "And wo unto them that seek deep to hide their counsel from the Lord! And their works are in the dark" (2 Nephi 27:27)	"The blood of the saints shall cry unto the Lord, because of secret combinations and works of darkness" (Mormon 8:27) "Why do ye build up your secret abominations to get gain?" (Mormon 8:40)

direct result of their having witnessed the destruction of the Nephites. With the Nephites destroyed and the Lamanites in a state of complete wickedness, it must have seemed clear to these ancient prophets that the fourth, main element of the Lehitic covenant—namely, that a remnant would be brought to knowledge of the covenant and become a righteous people—would not be accomplished within their lifetime. They had no recourse left but to send their record to a group of temporally distant Gentiles. Their hope, like the covenant itself, was *displaced* to a later generation; thus they sent a record to accompany and to facilitate that hope, a record containing instructions and warnings to the future arbiters of covenant fulfillment.

Helaman and Covenant Displacement

That Mormon paid careful attention to and had a deep comprehension of Nephi's threefold focus from 2 Nephi 26–27—on covenant displacement, the emergence of the record, and the role of secret combinations—is best exemplified in his editing of the book of Helaman.

Helaman 5 is the key chapter in this editorial work. It is the miraculous story of a small Lamanite conversion initiated by Nephi and Lehi—two sons of Helaman (to be distinguished from the Nephi and Lehi of the small plates)—within the confines of a prison. Nephi and Lehi, obeying a commission from their father to preach repentance (Helaman 5:6), seem to encounter wave after wave of failure[6] as they progress across the land, until their journey culminates in their being tossed into prison. Like Alma and Amulek before them (see Alma 14:17–29), the power of these missionaries was not inhibited by temporal restraints. Intent on killing their Nephite prisoners (Helaman 4:22), Lamanite guards enter the prison to find the two men conversing with angels, prompting a transcendent, elemental conversion of everyone in the prison, complete with dark clouds, fiery pillars, earthquakes, and angelic visitation. This

6. The text is not entirely clear on this point. A more nuanced view might hold that the text's silence regarding potential missionary success among the Nephites has been deliberately muted in order to highlight this conversion experience and to draw a sharper distinction between the Nephites and Lamanites, a theme that is particularly strong in Helaman.

small Lamanite contingent of converts proceeded to preach to their brethren until "the more part of the Lamanites were convinced of them, because of the greatness of the evidences which they had received. And as many as were convinced did lay down their weapons of war, and also their hatred and the tradition of their fathers" (Helaman 5:50–51).

I see two hands involved in this text: the original author and Mormon (as editor).[7] It seems clear that the original author understood this Lamanite conversion as the fulfillment of the Lehitic covenant and, as such, inscribed it into his narrative. This was accomplished by two main techniques: (1) allusions to major events in Nephite history and (2) symbolic parallels with Lehi's vision of the tree of life (1 Nephi 8).

The astute reader will notice almost immediately that Nephi's acquittal of the judgment seat (Helaman 5:4) echoes Alma's identical decision in Alma 4:15–19. Equally interesting is the concentration of important Book of Mormon characters mentioned *by name* (Helaman 5:9–12): King Benjamin, Amulek, Zeezrom, Ammon, and Limhi, not to mention the sources for the names of the two main characters, Nephi and Lehi.[8] Further allusions are made to Alma and Abinadi, as well (see table 2). By mentioning such potent figures and events in Nephite history, the author marks this event (Helaman 5) as the culimination, *the* event to which all others had merely been segues.

The author's second technique is more subtle, employing imagery that corresponds with Lehi's vision of the tree of life. Again, the names of Nephi and Lehi are crucial since they also refer back to the two founders of the Nephite nation, both of whom witnessed this vision. The most recognizable element common to the vision and Helaman 5 is the cloud of darkness that fills the prison (Helaman 5:28), analogous to the "mist of darkness" through which the masses made their way to the tree. Lehi's great and spacious building finds its parallel in the prison itself, which threatened to "tumble to the earth" (Helaman 5:31),

---

7. I recognize the distinct possibility that the original authorship of Helaman 5 could be attributed to Mormon, but it is ultimately the recontextualization of this chapter that is of importance to this paper.

8. Even more striking is that most of these figures had experienced at least one angelic visitation: King Benjamin in Mosiah 3:2, Amulek in Alma 10:7, and Ammon in Mosiah 27:8–11.

Table 2. Cataloging Nephite History

	Helaman 5	Reference
Gives Up Judgment-Seat	"Nephi had become weary because of their iniquity; and he yielded up the judgment-seat, and took it upon him to preach the word of God the remainder of his days" (Helaman 5:4)	"Alma . . . seeing all their inequality, began to be very sorrowful. . . . And he selected a wise man . . . and he was appointed chief judge. . . . He delivered the judgment-seat unto Nephihah" (Alma 4:15–19)
King Benjamin	"Remember, my sons, the words which king Benjamin spake unto his people; yea, remember that there is no other way nor means whereby man can be saved, only through the atoning blood of Jesus Christ" (Helaman 5:9)	"There shall be no other name given nor any other way nor means whereby salvation can come unto the children of men, only in and through the name of Christ" (Mosiah 3:17) "There is no other way or means whereby man can be saved, only in and through Christ" (Alma 38:9)
Amulek & Zeezrom	"Remember also the words which Amulek spake unto Zeezrom, in the city of Ammonihah; for he said unto him that the Lord surely should come to redeem his people, but that he should not come to redeem them in their sins, but to redeem them from their sins" (Helaman 5:10)	"And Zeezrom said again: Shall he save his people in their sins? And Amulek answered and said unto him: I say unto you he shall not. . . . He shall not save his people in their sins" (Alma 11:34–37)
Prison Type-Scene	"They were taken by an army of the Lamanites and cast into prison" (Helaman 5:21)	"Alma and Amulek answered him nothing; and he smote them again, and delivered them to the officers to be cast into prison" (Alma 14:17)
	". . . cast into prison; yea, even in that same prison in which Ammon and his brethren were cast by the servants of Limhi" (Helaman 5:21)	"They were surrounded by the king's guard, and were taken, and were bound, and were committed to prison" (Mosiah 7:7)

	Helaman 5	Reference
Angelic Message/ Earth Shaking	"Nephi and Lehi did stand forth and began to speak unto them, saying: Fear not, for behold, it is God that has shown unto you this marvelous thing . . . And behold, when they had said these words, the earth shook exceedingly" (Helaman 5:26–27)	"God sent his holy angel to stop us by the way. . . . And behold, he spake unto us, as if it were the voice of thunder, and the whole earth did tremble beneath our feet" (Alma 36:6–7)
Shining Faces	"The faces of Nephi and Lehi . . . did shine exceedingly" (Helaman 5:36)	"After Abinadi had spoken these words . . . his face shone with exceeding luster" (Mosiah 13:5)

just as the great and spacious building actually did. These parallels would mean little, however, if they did not include the most important element of the tree of life vision—the tree itself. Here the text supplies a "pillar of fire" (Helaman 5:43). Not only does the vertical linearity of a "pillar" evoke the image of a tree trunk, but the light and glory of fire is reminiscent of brilliant, white, almost luminescent fruit (1 Nephi 8:11). Cementing the parallel is the fact that, after Lehi reached the tree and tasted the fruit, his soul was "filled . . . with exceedingly great joy" (1 Nephi 8:12), language that is strikingly similar to the effect of the pillars of fire: the people within the prison "were filled with that joy which is unspeakable and full of glory" (Helaman 5:44–45).

Thus, while Lehi's original vision was tainted by the sting of Laman and Lemuel's rejection of the fruit (1 Nephi 8:17–18), a happier version comes some 550 years later when Laman and Lemuel, through their Lamanite descendants, gather at the root of the tree, beckoned through history (neatly cataloged in Helaman 5) by the fathers—two figures literally named Nephi and Lehi!—who now symbolically stand before them.

While the original author of Helaman 5 understood and portrayed this event as the miraculous and sublime fulfillment of the Lehitic

Table 3. Tree of Life Vision

	Helaman 5	Tree of Life Vision
Names	"Behold, my sons, . . . I have given unto you the names of our first parents who came out of the land of Jerusalem" (Helaman 5:6)	"[Lehi] spake unto us, saying: Behold, I have . . . seen a vision" (1 Nephi 8:2) "I [Nephi] had desired to know the things that my father had seen" (1 Nephi 11:1)
Metaphor	"Encircled about as if by fire" (Helaman 5:23) "Shine exceedingly, even as the faces of angels" (Helaman 5:36) "They were filled as if by fire" (Helaman 5:45)	"A large and spacious field, as if it had been a world" (1 Nephi 8:20)
Cloud of Darkness	"They were overshadowed with a cloud of darkness" (Helaman 5:28)	"There arose a mist of darkness; yea, even an exceedingly great mist of darkness" (1 Nephi 8:23)
Great and Spacious Building	"The walls of the prison did shake as if they were about to tumble to the earth" (Helaman 5:27) "Behold the earth shook exceedingly, and the walls of the prison trembled again, as if it were about to tumble to the earth" (Helaman 5:31)	"The great and spacious building . . . fell, and the fall thereof was exceedingly great" (1 Nephi 11:36)
Tree of Life	"The walls of the prison did shake as if they were about to tumble to the earth" (Helaman 5:27)	"I beheld a tree" (1 Nephi 8:10)
Fruit of the Tree	"They were filled with that joy which is unspeakable and full of glory. And behold, the Holy Spirit of God did come down from heaven, and did enter into their hearts, and they were filled" (Helaman 5:44–45)	"As I partook of the fruit thereof it filled my soul with exceedingly great joy; wherefore, I began to be desirous that my family should partake of it also" (1 Nephi 8:12)

covenant,[9] Mormon had the (dis)advantage of historical perspective. He understood that the brief righteousness manifested by the Lamanites in the wake of their Helaman 5 conversion did not qualify as a *full*-filment of the covenant, because secret combinations would eventually, by effecting the Nephite destruction, cut off the very possibility of true covenant fulfillment for the next fifteen hundred years. Mormon edited the book of Helaman to draw our attention away from, or at least to downplay the lasting significance of, the miraculous events of Helaman 5, and so to focus our attention on the problem of secret combinations.[10]

---

9. The Nephites generally most likely had a different understanding of the Lehitic covenant than we see evidenced by Nephi or Mormon. It is unknown how widely the writings of Nephi were circulated. Mormon himself wasn't aware of the small plates when he initially began his project, and only inserted them after his abridgment of the large plates was underway (Words of Mormon 1:3–5). Coupled with his historical vantage point, this must have influenced Mormon's thinking considerably. It is unlikely that the Nephites as a whole were so privileged. Throughout the book of Helaman, the emphasis is placed predominantly on the relationship between the Lamanites and the Nephites. The fulfillment of the covenant represented in Helaman 5 is followed by a period in which both peoples were righteous. If they were unaware of their future annihilation, the Nephites most likely interpreted the Lehitic covenant to imply a future utopia where the recently righteous Lamanites finally joined their always-fairly-righteous Nephite brethren. Again, Mormon had the advantage of historical perspective. When the Nephites were destroyed, that utopian possibility was eliminated, and thus Mormon's editing of Helaman began.

10. Mormon audiences are largely indebted to Ezra Taft Benson for their awareness of secret combinations: "In the Book of Mormon we find a pattern for preparing for the Second Coming. A major portion of the book centers on the few decades just prior to Christ's coming to America. . . . From the Book of Mormon we learn how disciples of Christ live in times of war. From the Book of Mormon we see the evils of secret combinations portrayed in graphic and chilling reality. . . . And more than anything else, we see in the Book of Mormon the dangers of materialism and setting our hearts on the things of the world. Can anyone doubt that this book was meant for us and that in it we find great power, great comfort, and great protection?" ("The Book of Mormon—Keystone of Our Religion," *Ensign*, November 1986, 4). A brief review of the literature available on the book of Helaman will demonstrate how well both President Benson and Mormon succeeded in shifting our attention in Helaman almost exclusively to secret combinations!

Mormon lessens the initial impact of Helaman 5 by surrounding the chapter with narratives about secret combinations. Chapters 1–2 deal with secret murders and contention for the judgment seat, eventually introducing Kishkumen, relating the formation of the Gadianton robber band, and describing their flight into the wilderness. After chapter 3 describes at great length the industrial endeavors and northward migration of the Nephites, chapter 4 regales us further with details about war and contention among the Nephites and Lamanites. That Helaman 5 is introduced only *after* all of this wickedness and destruction shows that the situation was not quite as benevolent as the original author of Helaman 5 thought. This is confirmed drastically when, in chapter 6 and immediately after the mass conversion, the Gadianton robbers suddenly return from their wilderness sojourn to take over the government. Helaman 5 is editorially sandwiched between narratives of violence and destruction initiated and perpetuated by secret combinations, and the effect on the reader is—or at least should be—the shock of realizing that it is secret combinations first and foremost that keep God's promises from being immediately fulfilled.

Shining Forth out of Darkness: The Role of the Book of Mormon

Having discussed the self-conscious nature of the small plates, argued for Mormon's editorial relationship to Nephi's encapsulation of that awareness, and explored the role of secret combinations in this story, I return, finally, to 2 Nephi 26–27, where we learn that one of the purposes of the Book of Mormon is to overturn secret combinations. 2 Nephi 27:24 introduces a significant change from Isaiah 29:13, the addressee suddenly becoming "him that *shall read* the words that shall be delivered." Verses 27 and 28 add "I will show unto" and "saith the Lord of Hosts," strengthening the emphasis that these are the words of the *Lord*. Nephi makes sure to emphasize that these words will come through a written record by changing the audience in verse 24 (as noted above) to create a framing parallel with Isaiah's retained language in verse 29 ("the words of the book"). In the intervening verses, he pronounces woe on "them that seek deep to hide their counsel" (presumably secret combinations) and foretells that "[he] know[s] all their works" (2 Nephi 27:27). To demonstrate this, the Lord announces a number of reversals: Lebanon will be made a fruitful field, the deaf will hear, the blind will see out of obscurity and darkness.

By addressing these deliverances to the reader of the Book of Mormon, the Lord demonstrates that it is the Book of Mormon itself that will effect the reversals. Foremost among them: the secret combinations Isaiah had described will be revealed and "brought to naught" (2 Nephi 27:31).

Language of reversal in connection with secret combinations in the Book of Mormon is not exclusive to Nephi, however. Alma 37:23 describes a stone that will "shine forth in *darkness* unto *light*," with the result that the Lord "may discover unto my people who serve me . . . the works of their brethren, yea, their secret works, their works of darkness." This verse also carries important implications for Joseph Smith's role as translator of the Book of Mormon. Also in verse 23, we find the name "Gazelem," a name employed as one of Joseph's code names in the early editions of the Doctrine and Covenants.[11] Regardless of whether or not the Gazelem of Alma 37:23 makes reference to a seer or a stone,[12] Joseph's adoption of the name implies that his role is *also* to "discover . . . secret works," a task, one could argue, that was accomplished primarily in the translation of the Book of Mormon.

11. D&C 78:9; 82:11; 104:26, 43, 45, 46. See Robin Scott Jensen, Robert J. Woodford, and Seven C. Harper, eds., *Revelations and Translations: Manuscript Revelation Books*, vol. 1 of the Revelations and Translations series of *The Joseph Smith Papers*, ed. Dean C. Jesse, Ronald K. Esplin, and Richard Lyman Bushman (Salt Lake City: Church Historian's Press, 2009), 267; Curt A. Bench, ed., *The Parallel Doctrine and Covenants* (Salt Lake City: Smith-Pettit Foundation, 2009), 149, 152, 204–5.

12. There is some ambiguity here, although the punctuation of the verse would seem to imply the latter. Royal Skousen offers compelling evidence for understanding Gazelem as the name of the servant (*Analysis of Textual Variants of the Book of Mormon* [Provo, UT: FARMS, 2007], 4:2361–63). For a possible etymology, see George Reynolds and Janne M. Sjodahl, *Commentary on the Book of Mormon*, 7 vols. (Salt Lake City: Deseret Book, 1955–61), 4:162. Like Skousen, Reynolds and Sjodahl agree that Gazelem is the name of the seer.

By far the most direct and explicit statement of this revelatory aspect of the Book of Mormon comes from the record itself. In Ether 8,[13] Moroni turns to his latter-day readers and offers a warning so crucial to his message that it deserves to be quoted in full:

> Wherefore, *O ye Gentiles,* it is wisdom in God that *these things should be shown unto you,* that thereby ye may repent of your sins, and suffer not that these *murderous combinations* shall get above you, which are built up to get power and gain—and the work, yea, even the work of destruction come upon you, yea, even the sword of the justice of the Eternal God shall fall upon you, to your overthrow and destruction if ye shall suffer these things to be.
>
> Wherefore, the Lord commandeth you, when ye shall see these things come among you that ye shall awake to a sense of your awful situation, because of this *secret combination* which shall be among you; or wo be unto it, because of the blood of them who have been slain; for they *cry from the dust*[14] for vengeance upon it, and also upon those who built it up. (Ether 8:23–24)

13. Like his father, Moroni also sees fit to include a narrative description of the formation of secret combinations. Ether 8 parallels Helaman in a number of linguistic and thematic ties: "Upheld" (Helaman 2:3; Ether 8:22), "exceedingly expert" (Helaman 2:4–5; Ether 8:8–12), "flatter" (Helaman 2:5; Ether 8:2), "gain power" (Helaman 2:8; Ether 8:16), "secret plan" (Helaman 2:8; Ether 8:9), "combination" (Helaman 2:8; Ether 8:18–24), "ye shall see" (Helaman 2:13; Ether 8:24), "the overthrow" (Helaman 2:13; Ether 8:23), a succession narrative/list of descent (Helaman 1:2; Ether 8:1), governmental contention (Helaman 1:2; Ether 8:2), flattery and cunning (Helaman 2:4–5; Ether 8:2), fathers succeeded/overcome by sons (Helaman 1:2; Ether 8:3–4), violent/subversive action takes place "by night" (Helaman 2:6; Ether 8:5), large-scale warfare (Helaman 1:17; Ether 8:5), the ruler is slain (Helaman 1:21; Ether 8:6), plans put into the "heart" (Helaman 2:8; Ether 8:17), covenant made (Helaman 2:3; Ether 8:14), "combination" is named (Helaman 2:8; Ether 8:18), ultimate destruction foreshadowed (Helaman 2:13; Ether 8:21).

14. It hardly needs commenting that Moroni is here making reference to Isaiah 29:4, quoted in 2 Nephi 26:16.

Neither Nephi nor Moroni let their message to latter-day Gentiles conclude on that note, however. Both point to a fuller purpose behind the covenant. In Ether 8:26, Moroni continues, "I . . . am commanded to write these things that evil may be done away, and that the time may come that Satan may have no power upon the hearts of the children of men, but that they may be persuaded to do good continually, that they may come unto the fountain of all righteousness and be saved." In 2 Nephi 27:33–34, the Lord goes on to inform us that, once secret combinations are completely overturned, Israel as a whole will be redeemed: "Thus saith the Lord, who redeemed Abraham, concerning the house of Jacob: Jacob shall not now be ashamed, neither shall his face now wax pale. But when he seeth his children, the work of my hands, in the midst of him, they shall sanctify my name, and sanctify the Holy One of Jacob, and shall fear the God of Israel." Secret combinations and works of darkness, like the Book of Mormon itself, are never far removed from the question of the covenant. Abraham and Jacob, the two patriarchs representative of the Lord's covenants with his people Israel, are always waiting at the conclusion of this chapter. The ultimate goal of the Lehitic covenant remains, as it always has been, to "land . . . souls at the right hand of God in the kingdom of heaven, to sit down with Abraham, and Isaac, and with Jacob, and with all our holy fathers, to go no more out" (Helaman 3:30), something that can only be accomplished as secret combinations are obliterated.

Nephi, Mormon, and Moroni, having seen the destruction caused by secret combinations and having their hopes dashed by these covert organizations, wrote their records to warn the future generation about the danger secret combinations pose to the fulfillment of the covenant. Standing on the edge of the temporal chasm that separated them from those future Gentiles who housed the hope of the Lehitic covenant, these ancient authors could do nothing more nor less than speak from the dust, alerting future readers to the marvelous gifts they offered: a record, a warning, and a covenant.

Appendix 1: Nephi's Text and Its Sources

Note: In this appendix we provide the base text of 2 Nephi 26–27 from which we worked. It serves two purposes. First, the base text employed is that of the 1920 edition of the Book of Mormon, but we have inserted, using standard editorial markings (deletions are marked by strikeout, e.g., ~~like this~~*, and insertions are marked with angle brackets, e.g., <like this>), whatever changes would need to be made to the 1920 text in order to bring it in line with what Royal Skousen's critical text project has brought to light. Second, footnotes are added not only to make clear what sources Nephi used in writing the text, but also to provide a handy reference tool by including the actual text of those sources in each footnote. Finally, italicized text in brackets [like this] is used to indicate sections of Nephi's text with significant connections to Isaiah 29 (the italics and brackets themselves, of course, are not in the 1920 edition). These connections are made clear in the source footnotes.*

2 Nephi 26

1 And after Christ shall have risen from the dead he shall show himself
unto you, my children, and my beloved brethren; and the words which
he shall speak unto you shall be the law which ye shall do.

2 For behold, I say unto you that I have beheld that many generations shall pass away, and there shall be great wars and contentions among my people.

3 And after the Messiah shall come there shall be signs given unto my people of his birth, and also of his death and resurrection; and great and terrible shall that day be unto the wicked, for they shall perish; and they perish because they cast out the prophets, and the saints, and stone them, and slay them; wherefore the cry of the blood of the saints shall ascend up to God from the ground against them.

4 Wherefore, all ~~those who~~ <they that> are proud, and that do wickedly, the day that cometh shall burn them up, saith the Lord of Hosts, for they shall be as stubble.[1]

5 And they that kill the prophets, and the saints, the depths of the earth shall swallow them up, saith the Lord of Hosts; and mountains shall cover them, and whirlwinds shall carry them away, and buildings shall fall upon them and crush them to pieces and grind them to powder.

6 And they shall be visited with thunderings, and lightnings, and earthquakes, and all manner of destructions, for the fire of the anger of the Lord shall be kindled against them,[2] and they shall be as stubble, and the day that cometh shall consume them, saith the Lord of Hosts.[3]

---

1. Malachi 4:1 (also cited at 1 Nephi 22:15): "For, behold, the day cometh, that shall burn as an oven; and all the proud, yea, and all that do wickedly, shall be stubble: and the day that cometh shall burn them up, saith the Lord of hosts, that it shall leave them neither root nor branch."

2. Isaiah 5:24–25 (also cited at 2 Nephi 15:24–25): "Therefore as the fire devoureth the stubble, and the flame consumeth the chaff, so their root shall be as rottenness, and their blossom shall go up as dust: because they have cast away the law of the Lord of hosts, and despised the word of the Holy One of Israel. Therefore is the anger of the Lord kindled against his people, and he hath stretched forth his hand against them, and hath smitten them: and the hills did tremble, and their carcases were torn in the midst of the streets. For all this his anger is not turned away, but his hand is stretched out still. And he will lift up an ensign to the nations from far, and will hiss unto them from the end of the earth: and, behold, they shall come with speed swiftly."

3. Malachi 4:1 (also cited at 1 Nephi 22:15): "For, behold, the day cometh, that shall burn as an oven; and all the proud, yea, and all that do wickedly, shall be stubble:

7 O the pain, and the anguish of my soul for the loss of the slain of my people! For I, Nephi, ~~have~~ <hath> seen it, and it well nigh consumeth me before the presence of the Lord; but I must cry unto my God: Thy ways are just.

8 But behold, the righteous that hearken unto the words of the prophets, and destroy them not, but look forward unto Christ with steadfastness for the signs which are given, notwithstanding all ~~persecution~~ <persecutions>—behold, they are they which shall not perish.

9 But the ~~Son~~ <Sun> of righteousness shall appear unto them; and he shall heal them,[4] and they shall have peace with him, until three generations shall have passed away, and many of the fourth generation shall have passed away in righteousness.

10 And when these things have passed away a speedy destruction cometh unto my people; for, notwithstanding the pains of my soul I have seen it; wherefore, I know that it shall come to pass; and they sell themselves for naught;[5] for, for the reward of their pride and their foolishness they shall reap destruction; for because they yield unto the devil and choose works of darkness rather than light, therefore they must go down to hell.

11 For the Spirit of the Lord will not always strive with man. And when the Spirit ceaseth to strive with man then cometh speedy destruction, and this grieveth my soul.

12 And as I spake concerning the convincing of the Jews, that Jesus is the very Christ, it must needs be that the Gentiles be convinced also that Jesus is the Christ, the Eternal God;

13 And that he manifesteth himself unto all those who believe in him, by the power of the Holy Ghost; yea, unto every nation, kindred, tongue, and people, working mighty miracles, signs, and wonders, among the children of men according to their faith.

---

and the day that cometh shall burn them up, saith the LORD of hosts, that it shall leave them neither root nor branch."

4. Malachi 4:2 (also cited at 2 Nephi 25:13): "But unto you that fear my name shall the Sun of righteousness arise with healing in his wings; and ye shall go forth, and grow up as calves of the stall."

5. Isaiah 52:3: "For thus saith the LORD, Ye have sold yourselves for nought; and ye shall be redeemed without money."

14 But behold, I prophesy unto you concerning the last days; concerning the days when the Lord God shall bring these things forth unto the children of men.

15 After my seed and the seed of my brethren shall have dwindled in unbelief, and shall have been smitten by the Gentiles; yea, [*after the Lord God shall have camped against them round about, and shall have laid siege against them with a mount, and raised forts against them; and after they shall have been brought down low in the dust*], even that they are not, yet the words of the righteous shall be written, and the prayers of the faithful shall be heard, and all those who have dwindled in unbelief shall not be forgotten.[6]

16 [*For those who shall be destroyed shall speak unto them out of the ground, and their speech shall be low out of the dust, and their voice shall be as one that hath a familiar spirit*]; for the Lord God will give unto him power, that he may whisper concerning them, even as it were [*out of the ground; and their speech shall whisper out of the dust*].[7]

17 For thus saith the Lord God: They shall write the things which shall be done among them, and they shall be written and sealed up in a book, and those who have dwindled in unbelief shall not have them, for they seek to destroy the things of God.

18 Wherefore, as those who have been destroyed have been destroyed speedily; [*and the multitude of their terrible ones shall be as chaff that passeth away—yea, thus saith the Lord God: It shall be at an instant, suddenly*]—[8]

19 And it shall come to pass, that those who have dwindled in unbelief shall be smitten by the hand of the Gentiles.

---

6. Isaiah 29:3-4: "And I will camp against thee round about, and will lay siege against thee with a mount, and I will raise forts against thee. / And thou shalt be brought down. . . ."

7. Isaiah 29:4: ". . . and shalt speak out of the ground, and thy speech shall be low out of the dust, and thy voice shall be, as of one that hath a familiar spirit, out of the ground, and thy speech shall whisper out of the dust."

8. Isaiah 29:5: "Moreover the multitude of thy strangers shall be like small dust, and the multitude of the terrible ones shall be as chaff that passeth away: yea, it shall be at an instant suddenly."

20 And the Gentiles are lifted up in the pride of their eyes, and have stumbled, because of the greatness of their stumbling block,[9] that they have built up many churches; nevertheless, they put down the power and <the> miracles of God, and preach up unto themselves their own wisdom and their own learning, that they may get gain and grind upon the face of the poor.[10]

21 And there are many churches built up which cause envyings, and strifes, and malice.

22 And there are also secret combinations, even as in times of old, according to the combinations of the devil, for he is the founder of all these things; yea, the ~~foundation~~ <founder> of murder; and works of darkness; yea, and he leadeth them by the neck with a flaxen cord, until he bindeth them with his strong cords forever.

23 For behold, my beloved brethren, I say unto you that the Lord God worketh not in darkness.

24 He doeth not anything save it be for the benefit of the world; for he loveth the world, even that he layeth down his own life that he may draw all men unto him. Wherefore, he commandeth none that they shall not partake of his salvation.

25 Behold, doth he cry unto any, saying: Depart from me? Behold, I say unto you, Nay; but he saith: Come unto me all ye ends of the earth, buy milk and honey, without money and without price.[11]

26 Behold, hath he commanded any that they should depart out of the synagogues, or out of the houses of worship? Behold, I say unto you, Nay.

27 Hath he commanded any that they should not partake of his salvation? Behold I say unto you, Nay; but he hath given it free for all

---

9. Isaiah 8:14–15 (also cited at 2 Nephi 18:14–15): "And he shall be for a sanctuary; but for a stone of stumbling and for a rock of offence to both the houses of Israel, for a gin and for a snare to the inhabitants of Jerusalem. And many among them shall stumble, and fall, and be broken, and be snared, and be taken."

10. Isaiah 3:15 (also cited at 2 Nephi 13:15): "What mean ye that ye beat my people to pieces, and grind the faces of the poor? saith the Lord God of hosts."

11. Isaiah 55:1 (also cited at 2 Nephi 9:50): "Ho, every one that thirsteth, come ye to the waters, and he that hath no money; come ye, buy, and eat; yea, come, buy wine and milk without money and without price."

men; and he hath commanded his people that they should persuade all men ~~to~~ <unto> repentance.

28 Behold, hath the Lord commanded any that they should not partake of his goodness? Behold I say unto you, Nay; but all men are privileged the one like unto the other, and none are forbidden.

29 He commandeth that there shall be no priestcrafts; for, behold, priestcrafts are that men preach and set themselves up for a light unto the world, that they may get gain and praise of the world; but they seek not the welfare of Zion.

30 Behold, the Lord hath forbidden this thing; wherefore, the Lord God hath given a commandment that all men should have charity, which charity is love. And except they should have charity they were nothing. Wherefore, if they should have charity they would not suffer the laborer in Zion to perish.

31 But the laborer in Zion shall labor for Zion; for if they labor for money they shall perish.

32 And again, the Lord God hath commanded that men should not murder; that they should not lie; that they should not steal; that they should not take the name of the Lord their God in vain; that they should not envy; that they should not have malice; that they should not contend one with another; that they should not commit whoredoms; and that they should <not> do none of these things; for whoso doeth them shall perish.

33 For none of these iniquities come of the Lord; for he doeth that which is good among the children of men; and he doeth nothing save it be plain unto the children of men; and he inviteth them all to come unto him and partake of his goodness; and he denieth none that come unto him, black and white, bond and free, male and female; and he remembereth the heathen; and all are alike unto God, both Jew and Gentile.

2 Nephi 27

1 But, behold, in the last days, or in the days of the Gentiles—yea, behold all the nations of the Gentiles and also the Jews, both those who shall come upon this land and those who shall be upon other lands,

yea, even upon all the lands of the earth, behold, they will be drunken with iniquity and all manner of abominations—

2 And when that day shall come [*they shall be visited of the Lord of Hosts, with thunder and with earthquake, and with a great noise, and with storm, and with tempest, and with the flame of devouring fire*].

3 [*And all the nations that fight against Zion, and that distress her, shall be as a dream of a night vision; yea, it shall be unto them, even as unto a hungry man which dreameth, and behold he eateth but he awaketh and his soul is empty; or like unto a thirsty man which dreameth, and behold he drinketh but he awaketh and behold he is faint, and his soul hath appetite; yea, even so shall the multitude of all the nations be that fight against Mount Zion*].[12]

4 For behold, all ye that ~~doeth~~ <do> iniquity, [*stay yourselves and wonder, for ye shall cry out, and cry; yea, ye shall be drunken but not with wine, ye shall stagger but not with strong drink*].[13]

5 [*For behold, the Lord hath poured out upon you the spirit of deep sleep. For behold, ye have closed your eyes, and ye have rejected the prophets; and your rulers, and the seers hath he covered because of your iniquity*].[14]

6 And it shall come to pass that the Lord God shall bring forth unto you the words of [*a book*], and they shall be the words of them which have slumbered.[15]

---

12. Isaiah 29:6–8 (for verses 2–3 taken together): "Thou shalt be visited of the LORD of hosts with thunder, and with earthquake, and great noise, with storm and tempest, and the flame of devouring fire. And the multitude of all the nations that fight against Ariel, even all that fight against her and her munition, and that distress her, shall be as a dream of a night vision. It shall even be as when an hungry man dreameth, and, behold, he eateth; but he awaketh, and his soul is empty: or as when a thirsty man dreameth, and, behold, he drinketh; but he awaketh, and, behold, he is faint, and his soul hath appetite: so shall the multitude of all the nations be, that fight against mount Zion."

13. Isaiah 29:9: "Stay yourselves, and wonder; cry ye out, and cry: they are drunken, but not with wine; they stagger, but not with strong drink."

14. Isaiah 29:10: "For the LORD hath poured out upon you the spirit of deep sleep, and hath closed your eyes: the prophets and your rulers, the seers hath he covered."

15. Isaiah 29:11: "And the vision of all is become unto you as the words of a book. . . ."

7 And behold the book shall be [*sealed*]; and in the book shall be a revelation from God, from the beginning of the world to the ending thereof.[16]

8 Wherefore, because of the things which are sealed up, the things which are sealed shall not be delivered in the day of the wickedness and abominations of the people. Wherefore the book shall be kept from them.

9 But the book shall be delivered unto a man, and he shall deliver the words of the book, which are the words of those who have slumbered in the dust, and he shall deliver these words unto another;

10 But the words which are sealed he shall not deliver, neither shall he deliver the book. For the book shall be sealed by the power of God, and the revelation which was sealed shall be kept in the book until the own due time of the Lord, that they may come forth; for behold, they reveal all things from the foundation of the world unto the end thereof.

11 And the day cometh that the words of the book which were sealed shall be read upon the house tops; and they shall be read by the power of Christ; and all things shall be revealed unto the children of men which ever have been among the children of men, and which ever will be even unto the end of the earth.

12 Wherefore, at that day when the book shall be delivered unto the man of whom I have spoken, the book shall be hid from the eyes of the world, that the eyes of none shall behold it save it be that three witnesses shall behold it, by the power of God, besides him to whom the book shall be delivered; and they shall testify to the truth of the book and the things therein.

13 And there is none other which shall view it, save it be a few according to the will of God, to bear testimony of his word unto the children of men; for the Lord God hath said that the words of the faithful should speak as if it were from the dead.

14 Wherefore, the Lord God will proceed to bring forth the words of the book; and in the mouth of as many witnesses as seemeth him good will he establish his word; and wo be unto him that rejecteth the word of God!

---

16. Isaiah 29:11: ". . . that is sealed. . . ."

15 But behold, it shall come to pass that the Lord God shall say
unto him to whom he shall deliver the book: Take these words which
are not sealed and [*deliver them to another, that he may show them unto
the learned, saying: Read this, I pray thee*]. And the learned shall say:
Bring hither the book, and I will read them.[17]
16 And now, because of the glory of the world and to get gain will
they say this, and not for the glory of God.
17 [*And the man shall say: I cannot bring the book, for it is sealed*].
18 [*Then shall the learned say: I cannot read it*].[18]
19 Wherefore it shall come to pass, that [*the Lord God will deliver
again the book and the words thereof to him that is not learned; and the
man that is not learned shall say: I am not learned*].[19]
20 Then shall the Lord God say unto him: The learned shall not
read them, for they have rejected them, and I am able to do mine own
work; wherefore thou shalt read the words which I shall give unto thee.
21 Touch not the things which are sealed, for I will bring them
forth in mine own due time; for I will show unto the children of men
that I am able to do mine own work.
22 Wherefore, when thou hast read the words which I have com-
manded thee, and obtained the witnesses which I have promised unto
thee, then shalt thou seal up the book again, and hide it up unto me,
that I may preserve the words which thou hast not read, until I shall see
fit in mine own wisdom to reveal all things unto the children of men.
23 For behold, I am God; and I am a God of miracles; and I will
show unto the world that I am the same yesterday, today, and forever;
and I work not among the children of men save it be according to their
faith.
24 And again it shall come to pass that [*the Lord shall say unto him
that shall read the words that shall be delivered him*]:[20]

---

17. Isaiah 29:11: ". . . which men deliver to one that is learned, saying, Read this, I pray thee. . . ."

18. Isaiah 29:11 (for verses 17–18 taken together): "and he saith, I cannot; for it is sealed."

19. Isaiah 29:12: "And the book is delivered to him that is not learned, saying, Read this, I pray thee: and he saith, I am not learned."

20. Isaiah 29:13: "Wherefore the Lord said. . . ."

25 [*Forasmuch as this people draw near unto me with their mouth, and with their lips do honor me, but have removed their ~~hearts~~ <heart> far from me, and their fear towards me is taught by the ~~precepts~~ <pre-cept> of men*]—[21]

26 [*Therefore, I will proceed to do a marvelous work among this people, yea, a marvelous work and a wonder, for the wisdom of their wise and learned shall perish, and the understanding of their prudent shall be hid*].[22]

27 [*And wo unto them that seek deep to hide their counsel from the Lord! And their works are in the dark; and they say: Who seeth us, and who knoweth us? And they also say: Surely, your turning of things upside down shall be esteemed as the potter's clay. But behold, I will show unto them, saith the Lord of Hosts, that I know all their works. For shall the work say of him that made it, he made me not? Or shall the thing framed say of him that framed it, he had no understanding?*][23]

28 [*But behold, saith the Lord of Hosts: I will show unto the children of men that it is not yet a very little while and Lebanon shall be turned into a fruitful field; and the fruitful field shall be esteemed as a forest*].[24]

29 [*And in that day shall the deaf hear the words of the book, and the eyes of the blind shall see out of obscurity and out of darkness*].[25]

---

21. Isaiah 29:13: ". . . Forasmuch as this people draw near me with their mouth, and with their lips do honour me, but have removed their heart far from me, and their fear toward me is taught by the precept of men."

22. Isaiah 29:14: "Therefore, behold, I will proceed to do a marvellous work among this people, even a marvellous work and a wonder: for the wisdom of their wise men shall perish, and the understanding of their prudent men shall be hid."

23. Isaiah 29:15–16: "Woe unto them that seek deep to hide their counsel from the LORD, and their works are in the dark, and they say, Who seeth us? and who knoweth us? Surely your turning of things upside down shall be esteemed as the potter's clay: for shall the work say of him that made it, He made me not? or shall the thing framed say of him that framed it, He had no understanding?"

24. Isaiah 29:17: "Is it not yet a very little while, and Lebanon shall be turned into a fruitful field, and the fruitful field shall be esteemed as a forest?"

25. Isaiah 29:18: "And in that day shall the deaf hear the words of the book, and the eyes of the blind shall see out of obscurity, and out of darkness."

30 [*And the meek also shall increase, and their joy shall be in the Lord, and the poor among men shall rejoice in the Holy One of Israel*].[26]

31 [*For assuredly as the Lord liveth they shall see that the terrible one is brought to naught, and the scorner is consumed, and all that watch for iniquity are cut off*];[27]

32 [*And they that make a man an offender for a word, and lay a snare for him that reproveth in the gate, and turn aside the just for a thing of naught*].[28]

33 [*Therefore, thus saith the Lord, who redeemed Abraham, concerning the house of Jacob: Jacob shall not now be ashamed, neither shall his face now wax pale*].[29]

34 [*But when he seeth his children, the work of my hands, in the midst of him, they shall sanctify my name, and sanctify the Holy One of Jacob, and shall fear the God of Israel*].[30]

35 [*They also that erred in spirit shall come to understanding, and they that murmured shall learn doctrine*].[31]

---

26. Isaiah 29:19: "The meek also shall increase *their* joy in the LORD, and the poor among men shall rejoice in the Holy One of Israel."

27. Isaiah 29:20: "For the terrible one is brought to nought, and the scorner is consumed, and all that watch for iniquity are cut off."

28. Isaiah 29:21: "That make a man an offender for a word, and lay a snare for him that reproveth in the gate, and turn aside the just for a thing of nought."

29. Isaiah 29:22: "Therefore thus saith the LORD, who redeemed Abraham, concerning the house of Jacob, Jacob shall not now be ashamed, neither shall his face now wax pale."

30. Isaiah 29:23: "But when he seeth his children, the work of mine hands, in the midst of him, they shall sanctify my name, and sanctify the Holy One of Jacob, and shall fear the God of Israel."

31. Isaiah 29:24: "They also that erred in spirit shall come to understanding, and they that murmured shall learn doctrine."

Appendix 2: Isaiah Appropriated

Note: This appendix provides the text of Isaiah 29 along with marginal notes explaining its method of appropriation in 2 Nephi 26–27.

1 Woe to Ariel, to Ariel, the city where David dwelt! add ye year to year; let them kill sacrifices.
2 Yet I will distress Ariel, and there shall be heaviness and sorrow: and it shall be unto me as Ariel.

3 And I will camp against thee round about, and will lay siege against thee with a mount, and I will raise forts against thee.
4 And thou shalt be brought down, and shalt speak out of the ground, and thy speech shall be low out of the dust, and thy voice shall be, as of one that hath a familiar spirit, out of the ground, and thy speech shall whisper out of the dust.
5 Moreover the multitude of thy strangers shall be like small dust, and the multitude of the terrible ones shall be as chaff that passeth away: yea, it shall be at an instant suddenly.

Submitted to a targumic expansion in 2 Nephi 26:15–18

6 Thou shalt be visited of the LORD of hosts with thunder, and with earthquake, and great noise, with storm and tempest, and the flame of devouring fire.

7 And the multitude of all the nations that fight against Ariel, even all that fight against her and her munition, and that distress her, shall be as a dream of a night vision.

8 It shall even be as when an hungry man dreameth, and, behold, he eateth; but he awaketh, and his soul is empty: or as when a thirsty man dreameth, and, behold, he drinketh; but he awaketh, and, behold, he is faint, and his soul hath appetite: so shall the multitude of all the nations be, that fight against mount Zion.

9 Stay yourselves, and wonder; cry ye out, and cry: they are drunken, but not with wine; they stagger, but not with strong drink.

10 For the LORD hath poured out upon you the spirit of deep sleep, and hath closed your eyes: the prophets and your rulers, the seers hath he covered.

Contextualized in 2 Nephi 27:2–5

11 And the vision of all is become unto you as the words of a book that is sealed, which men deliver to one that is learned, saying, Read this, I pray thee: and he saith, I cannot; for it is sealed:

12 And the book is delivered to him that is not learned, saying, Read this, I pray thee: and he saith, I am not learned.

Drastically expanded and systematically reworked, all according to a pattern of likening or typological interpretation, in 2 Nephi 27:6–23

13 Wherefore the Lord said, Forasmuch as this people draw near me with their mouth, and with their lips do honour me, but have removed their heart far from me, and their fear toward me is taught by the precept of men: 14 Therefore, behold, I will proceed to do a marvellous work among this people, even a marvellous work and a wonder: for the wisdom of their wise men shall perish, and the understanding of their prudent men shall be hid. 15 Woe unto them that seek deep to hide their counsel from the Lord, and their works are in the dark, and they say, Who seeth us? and who knoweth us? 16 Surely your turning of things upside down shall be esteemed as the potter's clay: for shall the work say of him that made it, He made me not? or shall the thing framed say of him that framed it, He had no understanding? 17 Is it not yet a very little while, and Lebanon shall be turned into a fruitful field, and the fruitful field shall be esteemed as a forest? 18 And in that day shall the deaf hear the words of the book, and the eyes of the blind shall see out of obscurity, and out of darkness. 19 The meek also shall increase their joy in the Lord, and the poor among men shall rejoice in the Holy One of Israel. 20 For the terrible one is brought to nought, and the scorner is consumed, and all that watch for iniquity are cut off: 21 That make a man an offender for a word, and lay a snare for him that reproveth in the gate, and turn aside the just for a thing of nought. 22 Therefore thus saith the Lord, who redeemed Abraham, concerning the house of Jacob, Jacob shall not now be ashamed, neither shall his face now wax pale. 23 But when he seeth his children, the work of mine hands, in the midst of him, they shall sanctify my name, and sanctify the Holy One of Jacob, and shall fear the God of Israel. 24 They also that erred in spirit shall come to understanding, and they that murmured shall learn doctrine.

Quoted in full in 2 Nephi 27:24–35

Appendix 3: Isaiah Edited

Note: This appendix puts Nephi's editorial expansion of Isaiah 29 on display by (1) presenting as a base text the KJV rendering of Isaiah 29 and then (2) inserting into that text modern editorial markings in order (3) to show in detail how Nephi has "edited" the text of Isaiah.

Deletions are marked by strikeout (e.g., ~~like this~~). Insertions are marked with angle brackets (e.g., <like this>). Bracketed ellipses (i.e., [. . .]) mark points where Nephi inserts a very large amount of material, enough to make it inconvenient to place the full insertion here.

~~1 Woe to Ariel, to Ariel, the city where David dwelt! add ye year to year; let them kill sacrifices.~~

~~2 Yet I will distress Ariel, and there shall be heaviness and sorrow: and it shall be unto me as Ariel.~~

(2 Nephi 26:15–18)

3 ~~And I will~~ <yea, after the Lord God shall have> camp<ed> against ~~thee~~ <them> round about, and ~~will~~ <shall have> la~~y~~<id> siege against ~~thee~~ <them> with a mount, and ~~I will~~ raise<d> forts against ~~thee~~ <them>.

4 And <after> ~~thou shalt be~~ <they shall have been> brought down <low in the dust, even that they are not, yet the words of the righteous shall be written, and the prayers of the faithful shall be heard, and all those who have dwindled in unbelief shall not be forgotten>, ~~and shalt~~ <for those who shall be destroyed shall> speak <unto them> out of the ground, and ~~thy~~ <their> speech shall be low out of the dust, and ~~thy~~ <their> voice shall be, as ~~of~~ one that hath a familiar spirit, <for the Lord God will give unto him power, that he may whisper concerning them, even as it were> out of the ground, and ~~thy~~ <their> speech shall whisper out of the dust.

5 <for thus saith the Lord God: They shall write the things which shall be done among them, and they shall be written and sealed up in a book, and those who have dwindled in unbelief shall not have them, for they seek to destroy the things of God. Wherefore, as those who have been destroyed have been destroyed speedily> ~~Moreover the multitude of thy strangers shall be like small dust,~~ and the multitude of the<ir> terrible ones shall be as chaff that passeth away: yea, <thus saith the Lord God> it shall be at an instant suddenly.

(2 Nephi 27:2–5)

6 <and when that day shall come> ~~Thou shalt~~ <they shall> be visited of the Lord of hosts with thunder, and with earthquake, and <with a> great noise, <and> with storm and tempest, and <with> the flame of devouring fire.

7 And ~~the multitude of~~ all the nations that fight against ~~Ariel~~ <Zion>, ~~even all that fight against her and her munition,~~ and that distress her, shall be as a dream of a night vision.

8 <yea> It shall even be <unto them even> as ~~when~~ <unto> ~~an~~ hungry man <which> dreameth, and, behold, he eateth; but he awaketh, and his soul is empty: or ~~as when~~ <like unto> a thirsty man <which> dreameth, and, behold, he drinketh; but he awaketh, and, behold, he is faint, and his soul hath appetite: <yea, even> so shall the multitude of all the nations be, that fight against mount Zion.

9 <for behold, all ye that do iniquity> Stay yourselves, and wonder; <for ye shall> cry ~~ye~~ out, and cry: <yea> ~~they are~~ <ye shall be> drunken, but not with wine; ~~they~~ <ye shall> stagger, but not with strong drink.

10 For <behold> the LORD hath poured out upon you the spirit of deep sleep, <for behold> ~~and hath~~ <ye have> closed your eyes: <and ye have rejected> the prophets and your rulers, <and> the seers hath he covered <because of your iniquity>.

(2 Nephi 27:6–23)

11 ~~And the vision of all is become unto you as~~ <and it shall come to pass that the Lord God shall bring forth unto you> the words of a book <and they shall be the words of them which have slumbered> ~~that is~~ <and behold the book shall be> sealed, [. . .] ~~which men~~ <take these words which are not sealed and> deliver <them> to ~~one~~ <another, that he may show them unto the> ~~that is~~ learned, saying, Read this, I pray thee: and ~~he saith~~ <the learned shall say: bring hither the book, and I will read them. and now, because of the glory of the world and to get gain will they say this, and not for the glory of God. and the man shall say>, I cannot <bring the book>; for it is sealed: <then shall the learned say: I cannot read it>

12 ~~And~~ <wherefore it shall come to pass, that the Lord God will deliver again> the book ~~is delivered~~ <and the words thereof> to him that is not learned, ~~saying, Read this, I pray thee~~: and ~~he saith~~, <the man that is not learned shall say> I am not learned. <then shall the Lord God say unto him> [. . .]

(2 Nephi 27:24–35)

13 ~~Wherefore~~ <and again it shall come to pass that> the Lord ~~said~~ <shall say unto him that shall read the words that shall be delivered him>, Forasmuch as this people draw near <unto> me with their mouth, and with their lips do honour me, but have removed their heart far from me, and their fear toward<s> me is taught by the precept of men:

14 Therefore, ~~behold~~, I will proceed to do a marvellous work among this people, <yea> ~~even~~ a marvellous work and a wonder: for the wisdom of their wise ~~men~~ <and learned> shall perish, and the understanding of their prudent ~~men~~ shall be hid.

15 <and> Woe unto them that seek deep to hide their counsel from the LORD, and their works are in the dark, and they say, Who seeth us? and who knoweth us?

16 <and they also say> Surely your turning of things upside down shall be esteemed as the potter's clay: <but behold, I will show unto them, saith the Lord of Hosts, that I know all their works> for shall the work say of him that made it, He made me not? or shall the thing framed say of him that framed it, He had no understanding?

17 <but behold, saith the Lord of Hosts: I will show unto the children of men that> ~~Is~~ it <is> not yet a very little while, and Lebanon shall be turned into a fruitful field, and the fruitful field shall be esteemed as a forest?

18 And in that day shall the deaf hear the words of the book, and the eyes of the blind shall see out of obscurity, and out of darkness.

19 The meek also shall increase <and> their joy <shall be> in the LORD, and the poor among men shall rejoice in the Holy One of Israel.

20 For <assuredly as the Lord liveth they shall see that> the terrible one is brought to nought, and the scorner is consumed, and all that watch for iniquity are cut off:

21 <and they> That make a man an offender for a word, and lay a snare for him that reproveth in the gate, and turn aside the just for a thing of nought.

22 Therefore thus saith the LORD, who redeemed Abraham, concerning the house of Jacob, Jacob shall not now be ashamed, neither shall his face now wax pale.

23 But when he seeth his children, the work of ~~mine~~ <my> hands, in the midst of him, they shall sanctify my name, and sanctify the Holy One of Jacob, and shall fear the God of Israel.

24 They also that erred in spirit shall come to understanding, and they that murmured shall learn doctrine.

Appendix 4: Cross-References

Note: Here we provide a comprehensive list of places where significant words and phrases from Isaiah 29:3–24 appear in 2 Nephi 25–30.

Isaiah 29:3

round about: 2 Nephi 25:6

Isaiah 29:4

down: 2 Nephi 25:16, 21, 29; 26:10, 15, 20, 24; 27:27, 28:15, 21; 30:12, 13
speak: 2 Nephi 25:1, 3, 5, 6, 8, 11, 18, 20, 27, 28; 26:1, 12; 27:12; 28:1; 29:8, 9, 11, 12; 30:1, 3
ground: 2 Nephi 26:3, 16; 28:10
dust: 2 Nephi 26:15, 16; 27:9
whisper: 2 Nephi 26:16; 28:22

Isaiah 29:5

terrible: 2 Nephi 26:3
passeth away: 2 Nephi 26:2, 9, 10; 30:6

Isaiah 29:6

visited: 2 Nephi 26:6; 28:16
Lord of hosts: 2 Nephi 26:4, 5, 6; 27:27, 28; 28:17
thunder: 2 Nephi 26:6
earthquake: 2 Nephi 26:6
fire: 2 Nephi 26:6; 28:23; 30:10

Isaiah 29:7

nations: 2 Nephi 25:3, 15, 16, 20, 22; 26:13; 27:1; 29:7, 8, 12; 30:8, 16
fight: 2 Nephi 25:14; 29:14

Isaiah 29:8

eateth: 2 Nephi 28:7, 8
drinketh: 2 Nephi 27:3; 28:7, 8
soul: 2 Nephi 25:4, 5, 13, 29; 26:7, 10, 11; 28:21
Zion: 2 Nephi 26:29, 30, 31; 27:3; 28:21, 24

Isaiah 29:9

wonder: 2 Nephi 25:17; 26:13
cry: 2 Nephi 26:3, 7, 25; 28:10, 25
drunken: 2 Nephi 27:1
spirit: 2 Nephi 25:4, 11; 26:11; 28:1

Isaiah 29:10

eyes: 2 Nephi 25:20; 26:20; 27:12; 30:6
prophets: 2 Nephi 25:5, 9, 18, 19, 28; 26:3, 5, 8
rulers: 2 Nephi 29:7
covered: 2 Nephi 26:5; 30:15

Isaiah 29:11

words: 2 Nephi 25:1, 3, 4, 5, 8, 18, 19, 22, 28; 26:1, 8, 15; 27:9, 10, 11, 13, 14, 15, 19, 20, 22, 24; 28:29; 29:2, 3, 7, 8, 9, 10, 11, 13, 14; 30:1, 3
book: 2 Nephi 26:17; 27:7, 8, 9, 10, 11, 12, 14, 15, 17, 19, 22; 28:2; 29:11; 30:3
sealed: 2 Nephi 26:17; 27:8, 10, 11, 15, 17, 21, 22; 30:3, 17
delivered: 2 Nephi 27:8, 9, 10, 12, 15, 19, 24
learned: 2 Nephi 25:4; 26:20; 27:15, 18, 19, 20; 28:4, 15, 30
read: 2 Nephi 27:11, 15, 18, 20, 22, 24

Isaiah 29:13

people: 2 Nephi 25:1, 3, 4, 5, 8, 14, 17, 18, 28; 26:2, 3, 7, 10, 13, 27; 27:8; 28:5; 29:1, 2, 4, 5, 14; 30:2, 6, 7, 8, 10
mouth: 2 Nephi 25:1; 27:14; 29:2; 30:9
lips: 2 Nephi 30:9
heart: 2 Nephi 25:10, 12, 13, 16, 27; 28:9, 13, 15, 20; 30:18
fear: 2 Nephi 28:8
taught: 2 Nephi 25:2, 5, 6, 28; 28:4, 9, 14
precept: 2 Nephi 28:5, 6, 14, 26, 30, 31

Isaiah 29:14

proceed: 2 Nephi 25:7, 17; 27:14; 29:1, 2, 4
marvelous work: 2 Nephi 25:17; 29:1
work: 2 Nephi 25:2, 17; 26:10, 13, 22, 23; 27:20, 21, 23; 28:5, 6, 9, 23; 29:1, 9, 11; 30:8, 17
people: 2 Nephi 25:1, 3, 4, 5, 8, 14, 17, 18, 28; 26:2, 3, 7, 10, 13, 27; 27:8; 28:5; 29:1, 2, 4, 5, 14; 30:2, 6, 7, 8, 10
wonder: 2 Nephi 25:17; 26:13
wisdom: 2 Nephi 26:20; 27:22; 28:30
wise: 2 Nephi 28:15
perish: 2 Nephi 25:21; 26:3, 8, 30, 31, 32; 28:16, 19; 30:1
understanding: 2 Nephi 25:1, 5, 8

Isaiah 29:15

seek: 2 Nephi 26:17, 29; 28:9; 29:5
hide: 2 Nephi 28:9
counsel: 2 Nephi 28:9, 30
works: 2 Nephi 25:2, 17; 26:10, 13, 22, 23; 27:20, 21, 23, 27; 28:5, 6, 9, 23; 29:1, 9, 11; 30:8, 17
dark: 2 Nephi 25:2; 26:10, 22, 23; 28:9; 30:6, 17
seeth: 2 Nephi 25:13; 26:7, 10; 27:22, 31
knoweth: 2 Nephi 25:1, 3, 5, 6, 7, 8, 23, 26, 27; 26:10; 27:27; 28:1; 29:7, 8; 30:4, 6, 16

Isaiah 29:16

surely: 2 Nephi 25:7; 28:1
work: 2 Nephi 25:2, 17; 26:10, 13, 22, 23; 27:20, 21, 23, 27; 28:5, 6, 9, 23; 29:1, 9, 11; 30:8, 17
understanding: 2 Nephi 25:1, 5, 8

Isaiah 29:18

day: 2 Nephi 25:7, 8, 12, 13, 16, 18; 26:3, 4, 6, 14; 27:1, 2, 8, 11, 12; 28:3, 6, 16, 20; 29:1; 30:18
hear: 2 Nephi 26:15; 28:5
words: 2 Nephi 25:1, 3, 4, 5, 8, 18, 19, 22, 28; 26:1, 8, 15; 27:9, 10, 11, 13, 14, 15, 19, 20, 22, 24; 28:29; 29:2, 3, 7, 8, 9, 10, 11, 13, 14; 30:1, 3

book: 2 Nephi 26:17; 27:7, 8, 9, 10, 11, 12, 14, 15, 17, 19, 22; 28:2; 29:11; 30:3
eyes: 2 Nephi 25:20; 26:20; 27:12; 30:6
see: 2 Nephi 25:13; 26:7, 10; 27:22, 31
darkness: 2 Nephi 25:2; 26:10, 22, 23; 28:9; 30:6, 17

Isaiah 29:19

meek: 2 Nephi 28:13; 30:9
poor: 2 Nephi 26:20; 28:13; 30:9
rejoice: 2 Nephi 25:26; 30:6
Holy One of Israel: 2 Nephi 25:29; 28:5; 30:2

Isaiah 29:20

terrible: 2 Nephi 26:3
nought: 2 Nephi 26:10
consumed: 2 Nephi 26:6, 7
iniquity: 2 Nephi 25:9, 12; 26:33; 27:1, 4, 5; 28:16

Isaiah 29:21

reproveth: 2 Nephi 30:9
turn: 2 Nephi 28:16
just: 2 Nephi 26:7; 28:16
a thing: 2 Nephi 28:16
nought: 2 Nephi 28:16

Isaiah 29:22

thus saith the Lord: 2 Nephi 26:17, 18; 28:30; 29:4
Abraham: 2 Nephi 29:14
face: 2 Nephi 26:20

Isaiah 29:23

seeth: 2 Nephi 25:13; 26:7, 10; 27:22, 31
children: 2 Nephi 25:6, 8, 17, 23, 26, 27; 26:1, 13, 14, 33; 27:11, 13, 21, 22, 23, 28; 28:2, 20, 30; 29:1, 7; 30:16, 18
work: 2 Nephi 25:2, 17; 26:10, 13, 22, 23; 27:20, 21, 23, 27; 28:5, 6, 9, 23; 29:1, 9, 11; 30:8, 17
hands: 2 Nephi 25:16, 17; 26:19; 28:6; 29:1; 30:6
name: 2 Nephi 25:13, 14, 16, 19, 20; 26:32
fear: 2 Nephi 28:8

Isaiah 29:24

erred: 2 Nephi 25:7, 20; 28:14
spirit: 2 Nephi 25:4, 11; 26:11; 28:1
understanding: 2 Nephi 25:1, 5, 8
murmured: 2 Nephi 29:8
learn: 2 Nephi 25:4; 26:20; 27:15, 18, 19, 20; 28:4, 15, 30
doctrine: 2 Nephi 28:9, 12, 15

Appendix 5: Further Reading

LDS Publications with Discussions of Isaiah 29 or 2 Nephi 26–27

Ball, Terry B., and Nathan Winn. *Making Sense of Isaiah: Insights and Modern Applications.* Salt Lake City: Deseret Book, 2009.

Brewster, Hoyt W. *Isaiah Plain and Simple: The Message of Isaiah in the Book of Mormon.* Salt Lake City: Deseret Book, 1995.

Brown, Samuel Morris. *In Heaven as It Is on Earth: Joseph Smith and the Early Mormon Conquest of Death.* New York: Oxford University Press, 2012.

Cloward, Robert A. "Isaiah 29 and the Book of Mormon." In *Isaiah in the Book of Mormon*, edited by Donald W. Parry and John W. Welch. Provo, UT: FARMS, 1998. 191–247.

Gardner, Brant A. *Second Witness: Analytical and Contextual Commentary on the Book of Mormon.* 6 vols. Salt Lake City: Kofford, 2007.

Gileadi, Avraham. *The Literary Message of Isaiah.* New York: Hebraeus Press, 1994.

Hullinger, Robert N. *Joseph Smith's Response to Skepticism.* Salt Lake City: Signature Books, 1992.

Ludlow, Victor L. *Isaiah: Prophet, Seer, and Poet.* Salt Lake City: Deseret Book, 1982.

———. *Unlocking Isaiah in the Book of Mormon*. Salt Lake City: Deseret Book, 2003.

McConkie, Joseph Fielding, and Robert L. Millet. *Doctrinal Commentary on the Book of Mormon*. 4 vols. Salt Lake City: Deseret Book, 1987.

Nibley, Hugh W. *Teachings of the Book of Mormon: Transcripts of Lectures Presented to an Honors Book of Mormon Class at Brigham Young University 1988–1990*. 4 vols. Provo, UT: FARMS, 1993.

Nyman, Monte S. *Great Are the Words of Isaiah*. Salt Lake City: Bookcraft, 1980.

———. *I Nephi Wrote This Record*. Orem, UT: Granite Publishing, 2004.

Parry, Donald W., Jay A. Parry, and Tina M. Peterson. *Understanding Isaiah*. Salt Lake City: Deseret Book, 1998.

Pratt, Orson. *Orson Pratt's Works*. Salt Lake City: Deseret News Press, 1945.

Quinn, D. Michael. *Early Mormonism and the Magic World View*. Salt Lake City: Signature Books, 1987.

Reynolds, George, and Janne M. Sjodahl. *Commentary on the Book of Mormon*. 7 vols. Salt Lake City: Deseret Book, 1955.

Skousen, Royal. *Analysis of Textual Variants of the Book of Mormon*. 6 vols. Provo, UT: FARMS, 2004–2009.

Sperry, Sidney B. *Book of Mormon Compendium*. Salt Lake City: Bookcraft, 1968.

Modern (Non-LDS) Isaiah Commentaries of Note

Barker, Margaret. "Isaiah." In *Eerdmans Commentary on the Bible*, edited by James D. G. Dunn and John W. Rogerson. Grand Rapids: Eerdmans, 2003. 489–542.

Beuken, William A. M. *Isaiah II*. Trans. Brian Doyle. Leuven, Belgium: Peeters, 2000.

Blenkinsopp, Joseph. *Isaiah 1–39: A New Translation with Introduction and Commentary*. NewYork: Doubleday, 2000.

Childs, Brevard S. *Isaiah*. Philadelphia: Westminster, 2000.

Conrad, Edgar W. *Reading Isaiah*. Minneapolis: Fortress, 1991.

Delitzsch, Friedrich. *Biblical Commentary on the Prophecies of Isaiah*. 2 vols. Edinburgh: T. & T. Clark, 1890.

Kaiser, Otto. *Isaiah 13–39: A Commentary.* Trans. R. A. Wilson. Philadelphia: Westminster, 1974.

McKinnon, Steven A., ed. *Ancient Christian Commentary on Scripture: Isaiah 1–39.* Downers Grove, IL: InterVarsity Press, 2004.

Motyer, J. Alec. *The Prophecy of Isaiah: An Introduction and Commentary.* Downers Grove, IL: InterVarsity Press, 1993.

Seitz, Christopher R. *Isaiah 1–39.* Louisville: John Knox Press, 1993.

Sweeney, Marvin A. *Isaiah 1–39, with an Introduction to Prophetic Literature.* Grand Rapids: Eerdmans, 1996.

Von Rad, Gerhard. *Old Testament Theology.* 2 vols. Trans. D. M. G. Stalker. New York: Harper & Row, 1965.

Watts, John D. *Isaiah 1–33.* Waco: Word Books, 1985.

Wildberger, Hans. *Isaiah 28–39.* Trans. Thomas H. Trapp. Minneapolis: Fortress, 2002.

Young, Edward J. *The Book of Isaiah.* 3 vols. Grand Rapids: Eerdmans, 1969.

Contributors

KIMBERLY M. BERKEY is a graduate student in philosophy of religion at Harvard Divinity School. Prior to graduate work, she studied as a Hinckley Scholar at Brigham Young University, and she has contributed several articles to Maxwell Institute publications, including *Studies in the Bible and Antiquity* and the *Journal of Book of Mormon Studies.*

JULIE A. P. FREDERICK teaches part-time in Brigham Young University's Department of Ancient Scripture. She earned an MA in comparative studies from BYU. She resides in Spanish Fork, Utah, with her husband, Nick, and their three children.

GEORGE B. HANDLEY is professor of interdisciplinary humanities and associate dean of the College of Humanities at Brigham Young University. He holds a PhD in comparative literature from the University of California, Berkeley. His publications include *Postslavery Literatures in the Americas* and *New World Poetics.* His current book project is tentatively entitled *From Chaos to Cosmos: Literature as Ecotheology.* He is also completing an environmentally themed novel entitled *American Fork.*

GRANT HARDY is professor of history and religious studies at the University of North Carolina at Asheville. He is the editor of *The Book of Mormon: A Reader's Edition* and the author of *Understanding the Book of Mormon: A Reader's Guide* along with two books on early Chinese history. His most recent publications include the *Oxford History of Historical Writing, Vol. 1*; *Great Minds of the Eastern Intellectual Tradition; and Sacred Texts of the World* (the last two are 36-lecture CD/DVD courses produced by the Teaching Company).

Heather Hardy earned an MBA from Brigham Young University and worked for several years in university administration at Yale and BYU before leaving the workforce to raise children and pursue a life of learning. She has published essays on the Book of Mormon in *Dialogue,* the *Journal of Book of Mormon Studies,* and *The Things Which My Father Saw: Approaches to Lehi's Dream and Nephi's Vision* (from the 40th Sperry Symposium at BYU). She resides with her husband, Grant Hardy, in Asheville, North Carolina.

Joseph M. Spencer received his PhD in philosophy from the University of New Mexico and is currently an adjunct instructor in the Department of Ancient Scripture at Brigham Young University. He is the author of *An Other Testament* and *For Zion*. He serves as the associate director of the Mormon Theology Seminar and as an associate editor of the *Journal of Book of Mormon Studies.*

Jenny Webb lives in Huntsville, Alabama, with her husband, Nick, and children. She has an MA in comparative literature from Brigham Young University and works as an editor and production manager for several academic journals. Her work on scripture has appeared in the volumes *Perspectives on Mormon Theology: Scriptural Theology* and *An Experiment on the Word: Reading Alma 32*. She is the current president of Mormon Scholars in the Humanities and serves on the Mormon Theology Seminar Executive Board.